Letters from Rifka

Karen Hesse

• • • •

With
Connected Readings

PRENTICE HALL
Upper Saddle River, New Jersey
Needham, Massachusetts

ISBN 0-13-437502-5

3 4 5 6 7 8 9 10   03 02 01 00

PRENTICE HALL

Acknowledgments

Grateful acknowledgment is made to the following for permission to reprint copyrighted material:

Ardis Publishers
"Prose and Poetry" and "Foreboding" by Alexander Pushkin from *Alexander Pushkin: Collected Narrative and Lyrical Poetry*, translated by Walter Arndt. Copyright © 1984 by Walter Arndt. Reprinted by permission of Ardis Publishers.

Bantam Books, a division of Random House, Inc.
From *Land of Promise* by Joan Lowery Nixon. Copyright © 1993 by Joan Lowery Nixon and Daniel Weiss Associates. Used by permission of Bantam Books, a division of Random House, Inc.

Georges Borchardt, Inc., for the author
"The Fields" from *Opening the Hand* by W. S. Merwin (New York: Atheneum, 1983). Copyright © 1983 by W. S. Merwin. Reprinted by permission of Georges Borchardt, Inc., for the author.

Nancy Smiler Levinson
"Mighty Woman with a Torch" from *I Lift My Lamp* by Nancy Smiler Levinson. Copyright © 1986 by Nancy Smiler Levinson. Reprinted by permission of the author. All rights reserved by the author.

Facts on File, Inc.
"Isaac Bashevis Singer" from *Ellis Island Interviews: In Their Own Words* by Peter Morton Coan. Copyright © 1997 by Peter Morton Coan. Reprinted by permission of Facts on File, Inc.

Franklin Watts, a division of Grolier Publishing
"Holding Onto My Cultural Identity" from *Newcomers to America* by Judith Greenberg. Copyright © 1996 by Judith E. Greenberg. Reprinted by permission of Franklin Watts, a division of Grolier Publishing.

HarperCollins Publishers, Inc.
"A Nation of Nations" from *A Nation of Immigrants* by John F. Kennedy. Copyright © 1964 by Anti-Defamation League of B'nai B'rith. Reprinted by permission of HarperCollins Publishers, Inc.

(Acknowledgments continue on p. 156.)

Contents

Letters from Rifka

Historical Note

IN the years surrounding World War I, many people living in Eastern Europe found it difficult to feed and clothe their families. War made supplies short and conditions were often intolerable. National borders shifted back and forth, splitting families apart, increasing their suffering. These struggles led to frustration and anger.

The impoverished peasants of Russia endured great hardships while the government far above them crumbled with the ousting of the czar. To ease the mounting pressure, the government placed agents in the villages and towns of Russia. These agents intentionally stirred up trouble, diverting the peasants' anger away from the government and directing it toward the Jews. Peasants, infected with a mob fever that produced the pogroms, swept through Jewish settlements breaking windows, looting, burning, beating, and murdering the unfortunates in their path.

During this period in Russian history, many restrictions were borne on the shoulders of the Jewish people. They were denied the right to earn a living at most professions. Travel beyond their ghettos or settlements was forbidden without proper government paperwork, which was often either slow in coming or denied altogether. Jews could not own property, nor were they allowed to have in their possession more than two of any given object.

Many Russians sought to drive Jews from the country permanently by making their lives wretched. In the Russian Army, Jewish boys were assigned the least desirable tasks. Often, if they survived the perils of their assignments, if they survived the inadequate provisions supplied them, they were tortured or killed by their own comrades, the non-Jewish soldiers they served beside.

This climate drove thousands and thousands of families from their homelands—not just Jews, but many others as well. In search of a better life, those families sought sanctuary in countries across the globe. We, today, are the beneficiaries of their legacy of courage and determination.

Author's Note

WHEN I began this book, I set out to write about my family's migration from Russia to the United States. I recalled a story about my grandmother wearing white kid gloves as she rode through Poland in the back of an oxcart. I remembered the tale of my grandfather, denied passage on the *Titanic* because he was "only an immigrant." But that's all I remembered.

I phoned my mother and my aunts for help. They contributed a wealth of stories about their own childhood, but they couldn't shed much light on the family history.

"Call your great-aunt Lucy," my mother suggested.

I barely remembered Aunt Lucy. I pictured a frail, eighty-year-old woman. To my surprise, the voice on the other end of the line resounded with strength, steadiness, and humor.

"Certainly I'll help you," she said. "What do you want to know?"

I sent Aunt Lucy a list of questions in the mail. She shot me back a tape on which she spoke at breakneck speed for five breathless minutes. I remember holding on to the handle of my tape player, feeling like a passenger on a roller coaster as I listened to Aunt Lucy's account of her journey to America. When she signed off, the hiss and crackle of blank tape taunted me.

I phoned Aunt Lucy again. "I've listened to your tape," I said. "I think I need to see you."

She laughed as if she'd known I was coming all along.

Two months later, on a steamy East Coast afternoon, with my head full of research, I arrived on Aunt Lucy's doorstep.

Greeting me was a tiny woman with an unruly bun of snow-white hair on the top of her head. She welcomed me into her home and into her past.

Letters from Rifka draws largely on the memories of Lucy Evrutin. I have changed names and adjusted certain details, but this story is, above all else, Aunt Lucy's story.

Letters from Rifka

Karen Hesse

... and from
The gloomy land of lonely exile
To a new country bade me come. ...
—*Pushkin*

September 2, 1919
Russia

My Dear Cousin Tovah,
We made it! If it had not been for your father, though, I think my family would all be dead now: Mama, Papa, Nathan, Saul, and me. At the very best we would be in that filthy prison in Berdichev, not rolling west through Ukraine on a freight train bound for Poland.

I am sure you and Cousin Hannah were glad to see Uncle Avrum come home today. How worried his daughters must have been after the locked doors and whisperings of last night.

Soon Bubbe Ruth, my dear little grandmother, will hear of our escape. I hope she gives a big pot of Frusileh's cream to Uncle Avrum. How better could she thank him?

When the sun rose above the trees at the train station in Berdichev this morning, I stood alone outside a boxcar, my heart knocking against my ribs.

I stood there, trying to look older than my twelve years. Wrapped in the new shawl Cousin Hannah gave to me, still I trembled.

"Wear this in health," Hannah had whispered in my ear as she draped the shawl over my shoulders early this morning, before we slipped from your house into the dark.

"Come," Papa said, leading us through the woods to the train station.

I looked back to the flickering lights of your house, Tovah.

"Quickly, Rifka," Papa whispered. "The boys, and Mama, and I must hide before light."

"You can distract the guards, can't you, little sister?" Nathan said, putting an arm around me. In the darkness, I could not see his eyes, but I felt them studying me.

"Yes," I answered, not wanting to disappoint him.

At the train station, Papa and Mama hid behind bales of hay in boxcars to my right. My two giant brothers, Nathan and Saul, crouched in separate cars to my left. Papa said that we should hide in different cars. If the guards discovered only one of us, perhaps the others might still escape.

Behind me, in the dusty corner of a boxcar, sat my own ruck-sack. It waited for me, holding what little I own in this world. I had packed Mama's candlesticks, wrapped in my two heavy dresses, at the bottom of the sack.

Your gift to me, the book of Pushkin, I did not pack. I kept it out, holding it in my hands.

I would have liked to fly away, to race back up the road, stopping at every door to say good-bye, to say that we were going to America.

But I could not. Papa said we must tell no one we were leaving, not even Bubbe Ruth. Only you and Hannah and Uncle Avrum knew. I'm so glad at least you knew, Tovah.

As Papa expected, not long after he and Mama and the boys had hidden themselves, two guards emerged from a wooden shelter. They thundered down the platform in their heavy boots, climbing in and out of the cars, making their search.

They did not notice me at first. Saul says I am too little for anyone to notice, but you know Saul. He never has a nice word to say to me. And I am small for a girl of twelve. Still, my size did not keep the guards from noticing me. I think the guards missed seeing me at first because they were so busy in their search of the train. They were searching for Nathan.

You know as well as I, Tovah, that when a Jewish boy deserts the Russian Army, the army tries hard to find him. They bring him back and kill him in front of his regiment as a warning to the others. Those who have helped him, they also die.

Late last night, when Nathan slipped away from his regiment and appeared at our door, joy filled my heart at seeing my favorite brother again. Yet a troubled look worried Nathan's face. He hugged me only for a moment. His dimpled smile vanished as quickly as it came.

"I've come," he said, "to warn Saul. The soldiers will soon follow. They will take him into the army."

I am ashamed, Tovah, to admit that at first hearing Nathan's news made me glad. I wanted Saul gone. He drives me crazy.

From his big ears to his big feet, I cannot stand the sight of him. Good riddance, I thought.

How foolish I was not to understand what Nathan's news really meant to our family.

"You should not have come," Mama said to Nathan. "They will shoot you when you return."

Papa said, "Nathan isn't going to return. Hurry! We must pack!" We all stared at him.

"Quickly," Papa said, clapping his hands. "Rifka, run and fill your rucksack with all of your belongings." I do not know what Papa thought I owned.

Mama said, "Rifka, do you have room in your bag for my candlesticks?"

"The candlesticks, Mama?" I asked.

"We either take them, Rifka, or leave them to the greedy peasants. Soon enough they will swoop down like vultures to pick our house bare," Mama said.

Papa said, "Your brothers in America have sent for us, Rifka. It is time to leave Russia and we are not coming back. Ever."

"Don't we need papers?" I asked.

Papa looked from Nathan to Saul. "There is no time for papers," he said.

Then I began to understand.

We huddled in your cellar through the black night, planning our escape. Uncle Avrum only shut you out to protect you, Tovah.

Hearing the guards speak this morning, I understand his precaution. It was dangerous enough for you to know we were leaving. We could not risk telling you the details of our escape in case the soldiers came to question you.

The guards were talking about Nathan. They were saying what they would do to him once they found him, and what they would do to anyone who had helped him.

Nathan hid under a stack of burlap bags, one boxcar away from me. I knew, no matter how frightened I was, I must not let them find Nathan.

The guards said terrible things about our family. They did not know me, or Mama or Papa. They did not even know Nathan, not really. They could never have said those things about my brother Nathan if they knew him. Saul, maybe, clumsy-footed Saul. They could have said hateful things about Saul, but never Nathan. The guards spoke ill of us, not because of anything we had done, not because of anything we had said. Just because we were Jews. Why is it, Tovah, that in Russia, no matter what the trouble, the blame always falls upon the Jews?

The guards' bayonets plunged into bales and bags and crates in each boxcar. That is how they searched, with the brutal blades of their bayonets. The sound of steel in wood echoed through the morning.

I stood trembling in the dawn, Tovah, gripping your book in my hands to steady myself. I feared the guards would guess from one look at me what I was hiding.

For just a moment, I glanced toward the cars where Mama and Papa hid, to gather courage from them. My movement must have caught the guards' attention.

"You!" I heard a voice shout. "You there!"

The guards hastened down the track toward me. One had a rough, unshaven face and a broad mouth. He stared at me for a moment or two as if he recognized me. Then he seemed to change his mind. He reached out to touch my hair.

This is what Papa hoped for, I think. People have often stopped in wonder at my blond curls.

You say a girl must not depend on her looks, Tovah. It is better to be clever. But as the guards inspected me, from the worn toes of my boots to my hair spilling out from under my kerchief, I hoped my looks would be enough.

I hated the guard touching my hair. I clutched your book of poetry tighter to keep my hands from striking him away. I knew I must not anger him. If I angered him, I not only put my life in danger, I endangered Mama and Papa and Nathan and Saul, too.

The guard with the unshaven face held my curls in his hand. He looked up and down the length of me as if he were hungry and I were a piece of Mama's pastry. I held still. Inside I twisted like a wrung rag, but on the outside I held still.

Papa is so brave, the guards would not frighten him. I remember the time soldiers came to our house and saw on Papa's feet a new pair of boots. Uncle Shlomo had made them for Papa from leftover pieces of leather. The soldiers said, "Take the boots off. Give them here." Papa refused. The soldiers whipped Papa, but still Papa refused to hand over his boots. They would have killed Papa for those boots, but their battalion marched into sight. The soldiers hit Papa once more, hard, so that he spit blood, but they left our house empty-handed.

This was the courage of my papa, but how could he ever think I had such courage?

Courage or not, of all my family, only I could stand before the Russian soldiers, because of my blond hair and my blue eyes.

Papa, Mama, and the boys, they all have the dark coloring and features of the Jews. Only I can pass for a Russian peasant.

And of course, as you know, Tovah, of all my family, only I can speak Russian without a Yiddish accent. Uncle Avrum calls it my "gift" for language. What kind of gift is this, Tovah?

The guard ran his greasy fingers through my curls. He smelled of herring and onion.

"Why aren't you on your way to school?" he demanded.

My heart beat in my throat where my voice should have been. Mama is always saying my mouth is as big as the village well. Even you, Tovah, tell me I should not speak unless I have something to say. I know I talk too much. Yet as the guard played with my hair, fear silenced me.

"Who are you?" he asked. "What are you doing here?"

I forced myself to answer. I spoke in Russian, making my accent just like Katya's, the peasant girl who comes to light our Sabbath fire.

"I'm here," I said, "to take the train. My mother has found me work in a wealthy house."

"You are young to leave home," the rough-faced guard said, brushing the ends of my hair across his palm. "And such a pretty little thing."

"That's just what I told my mother," I said. "But she insisted that I go anyway."

The guard laughed. "Maybe you should stay in Berdichev. I might have better work for you here."

"Maybe I will," I said, looking into his rough, ugly face.

Papa did not tell me what to say to the guards. He simply said to distract them.

If it had been just the one guard, I might have occupied him until the train left the station.

Only there was another guard. He had a thin face and a straight back. His eyes were like the Teterev in the spring when the snow melts, churning with green ice. My curls did not interest him.

"Let her go," the thin guard ordered. "Search the boxcars around and behind her."

My heart banged in my throat.

I had to keep the guards away from my family until Uncle Avrum arrived from the factory. I prayed for Uncle Avrum to come soon.

Tovah, I tried to do what you are always telling me. I tried to be clever.

"You are in the army, aren't you?" I said. "I know all about soldiers in the army."

The guard with the eyes of green ice stared hard at me. "Tell me what you know," he demanded.

"Well," I said. "When I was nine, I saw some soldiers from Germany. Did you ever see those German soldiers?"

Both of the guards looked as if they remembered the Germans well.

"Those Germans came in airplanes," I said. "So noisy, those planes." I clasped my hands over my ears, banging myself with your book of Pushkin.

The stiff-backed guard glared at me.

"There was a German pilot," I said. "A German pilot with a big potbelly. I wondered how he could fit in his plane; such a small plane, such a big German."

The thin guard pivoted away from me. He squinted at something moving in the bushes across the train yard. Lifting his rifle, he aimed at the bushes and fired. Two birds rose noisily into the air.

I started talking faster.

"That German liked me pretty well," I said. "He bought me candy and took me for walks. One day he put me in his plane and started the propeller. I didn't like that, so I jumped out."

I knew I was talking too fast. When I talked like this at home, Saul always got annoyed with me.

I couldn't make myself slow down. The words came spilling out. If I could just keep them listening, they would run out of time to search the train.

"I jumped out of that fat German's plane and landed in the mud," I said. "And I ran home like the devil was chasing me. The German called for me to stop, but I wasn't stopping for him. I—"

"Enough!" the thin guard commanded. "Enough of your chatter." He pushed me aside and climbed into the freight car behind me. He sank his bayonet into the hay bales inside the car.

I asked the guard with the rough beard, "What is the problem? What is he looking for?" I tried to keep my voice from betraying my fear.

Suddenly the guard reappeared in the doorway to the freight car with my rucksack dangling from his bayonet. "What is this?"

I thought, If he finds Mama's candlesticks in my rucksack, it is all over for my entire family. "I can't go without my belongings, can I?" I said.

The two guards started arguing.

"Leave the girl alone," said the one with the rough beard. "She's a peasant, farmed out by her mother."

The other narrowed his eyes. "She's hiding something," he said.

"What could she hide?"

The thin guard glared at me again. "This is very heavy for clothing," he said, swinging my rucksack at the end of his bayonet. "What have you got in here?"

"What do you think?" said the guard with the rough face. "You think she's hiding a Jew in her rucksack? You think she has something to do with the Nebrot boy? Look at her, listen to her. She's no Jew."

The other guard jumped down from the car, tossing my rucksack on the ground. My bag hit with a thud.

"What's in there?" he asked again, preparing to rip my bag open with the razor-sharp blade of his bayonet.

"Books," I said. "Like this one." I held up your Pushkin, Tovah. "I like to read."

The guard hesitated, staring into my face, but he did not rip open my rucksack. He started instead toward the next car, the car with Nathan inside. I did not know how to stop him.

That is when your father arrived, Tovah. It had taken him longer at the factory than he'd expected.

"Guards! Come here!" Uncle Avrum shouted from the woods.

The guards turned toward his voice. I turned too. The trees on either side of the road dwarfed Uncle Avrum. He stood short and round with his red beard brushing the front of his coat. I knew the smell of that coat.

He and Papa and Mama had planned for this. Mama had hoped not to involve your father, but Uncle Avrum insisted on being part of the plan. He would make certain the guards suspected nothing. He said Papa could not let the fate of our entire family rest on the shoulders of a child.

I did not like when he talked about me that way last night, calling me a child. I felt insulted. Yet when I heard him call out to the guards this morning, all I felt was relief.

"Guards!" Uncle Avrum shouted again. "My factory. Someone broke into my factory." He is a good actor, your father, in case you didn't know.

The guards squinted their eyes against the morning sun. They recognized Uncle Avrum, but the thin guard did not want to help him.

"We must inspect this entire train before it leaves the station," he said to the guard beside him. "That man is only a Jew. Why bother with the troubles of a Jew?"

The guard with the unshaven face hesitated.

"We might get in trouble if we don't help him. That's Avrum

Abromson. I once carried a message to him at his factory. He has important friends."

"Come!" Uncle Avrum demanded. "Hurry! I haven't got all day."

I thought they would shoot Uncle Avrum for speaking to them in that way. They certainly would have shot Papa. But Uncle Avrum's demand seemed to make up their minds to go with him. I knew your family had influence, Tovah, but I never realized how much. The guards left me by the train and headed across the clearing toward your father and his factory. I prayed Uncle Avrum had made the robbery look real so they would not suspect him.

The train whistle blew, once, twice, as the rough-bearded guard and Uncle Avrum disappeared up the road. The thin guard turned back toward me, looking for a moment as if he might change his mind and return to finish the inspection. Then he, too, vanished into the woods.

The train, straining on the tracks, moved a little backward before it started rolling forward, slowly, out of Berdichev.

You know what a good runner I am. I have learned to run to keep out of Saul's reach. Outrunning the train was easy. I heaved my rucksack from the ground, tossing it into the boxcar. Stones skipped out from under my boots as I scrambled alongside, jumped on board, and, sprawling on my belly, pulled myself in.

Quickly I tucked into the shadows of the car so no one could see me. The freight car smelled warm and rich, like cattle, and I thought of Bubbe Ruth's sweet cow Frusileh.

I write this letter to you with my good school pencil in the blank pages at the front of your Pushkin. I am writing very neat and tiny so as not to spoil the book. I hope you do not mind that I am writing in your book, Tovah, but I have no other paper. I know this letter can never reach you, but in writing to you, I feel less frightened. You have been a big sister and a best friend to me. I cannot bear to think of never talking to you again. So I will talk to you by writing about my journey.

We are heading for the Polish border. That is all I know. I cannot even speak the language. What will it be like in Poland, and beyond that, in America, where at last I will meet my three oldest brothers? I can hardly believe that I too will soon live in such a place as America.

Shalom, my little house. Shalom, my family; shalom, Berdichev, and my dear little grandmother, Bubbe Ruth. Shalom, Hannah and Aunt Anna and Uncle Avrum, but most of all Tovah,

Shalom to you,
Rifka

... And with a sword he clove my breast,
Plucked out the heart he made beat higher,
And in my stricken bosom pressed
Instead a coal of living fire. ...

— *Pushkin*

September 3, 1919
Poland

Dear Tovah,

We were fortunate that we ran into no further trouble until we reached the Polish border. At the border, though, guards came aboard.

"Get off the train!" a squat man ordered. His round face and red cheeks did not match the sharpness of his voice.

"Get all your things out of the train! Take off your clothes. A doctor must examine you before you enter Poland."

Can you imagine? Taking off your clothes just like that in the middle of a train yard? Tovah, doctors examine you often because of your crooked back. Is this the way they treat you?

I fought them. I would not take off my clothes for them.

"Do as I say!" the guard barked at me. "Or you will be sent back, all of you."

From the fierceness of his voice I knew he would not hesitate to turn us over to the Russian police.

I could not have my family returned to Berdichev because of me. I took off my clothes.

I huddled beside Mama as we stood in our underwear in the waning daylight outside the boxcar. Aunt Rachel had made this underwear for me. It was white cotton and very pretty. She had made me two sets, but one was stolen from me as I swam in the Teterev this past summer.

I thought of the things the Russians had taken from my family as I stood in the train yard and I was angry. Why, Tovah? Why is it that if a Russian peasant does not get what he wants, he feels justified in stealing it from a Jew?

Papa and the boys undressed on the opposite side of the car. At least they allowed us that much privacy.

Mama and I, we had folded our clothes on top of our bags in the dry grass along the track. The guards picked up our clothes and our belongings and took them away. Even my rucksack with Mama's candlesticks.

Before I could yell to them to bring our things back, the doctor came.

He growled at us. I could not understand his words, but he made it clear what he wanted. He ordered us to remove our underwear.

This doctor, he stank of vomit and schnapps. His breath choked my throat and I thought I would be sick. Mama did not seem to notice his stench. She smiled and nodded to him. Perhaps she feared he would send us back to Russia. Why else would she act so?

Mama helped me to remove my underwear, shielding my body with her own. Her gold locket hung between her breasts. "Keep quiet for once, Rifka," she whispered in my ear. "Stay behind me."

I covered my nakedness with my hands as best I could, but Mama, she acted as if stripping before the Polish doctor was no trouble, like we did this every day. She pretended this, I think, to protect me.

The doctor examined us. He look longer with Mama. I could hardly believe this brave woman was the same who wept with fear in your cellar last night. The doctor spent so much time with Mama, he hardly noticed me.

When he did turn his attention to me, the way he looked gave me gooseflesh. Tovah, you are so practical. You will say I had gooseflesh because we stood naked outside in the cold, but it was not the cold that caused me to shiver.

The doctor made me feel dirty. He looked in my eyes and my mouth and my hair. "Are you sick?" he asked me in Russian.

I kept my eyes down. I could not stand to look at him. I stared instead at my toes curled tight in the stones at the edge of the tracks. I prayed the doctor would just go away.

He yelled at me, something in Polish. Mama spoke with him.

Then she took my hand and led me into a small building. In the building, a woman sprayed us with something vile. It burned my skin and my scalp, my nose and my eyes.

Finally the Polish guards allowed us back onto the train. They returned our clothes to us and our bags, stinking of fumigation. My eyes watered from the stench of it.

That was not the worst, though. When I lifted my rucksack, it was not as heavy as it had been before. I searched the entire bag, emptying it out on the floor of the train, but Mama's candlesticks were gone.

"So they stole our candlesticks," Mama said. "It could be worse, Rifka, much worse. Stop sniffling and finish getting dressed."

We pulled our clothes back on before Papa and Nathan and Saul joined us. Mama sighed with relief as they climbed into the car.

I turned away from their nakedness. How could the Poles do this to my papa, to my brothers? How could the Poles do this to me?

The train started moving before Papa and the boys finished dressing. That is how we entered Poland.

I have never been in another country before, not even in another village. You know how the Russians kept us, Tovah, like prisoners, never permitting us to travel. Russia has not been so bad for you. With money, Russia can be very good, even for a Jew. For us it was a prison.

Poland does not look that different from Berdichev. The same crooked cottages, the same patchy roads, the same bony fences leaning into the dust. Looking out from the train, we see people dressed like us, in browns and blacks; people wrapped in layers of clothes. The women bundle their heads in kerchiefs, the men shuffle along in ankle coats and boots. Will it be like this in America too?

I will stop writing for now. My head throbs and my body aches from all that has happened.

> *Shalom, my cousin,*
> *Rifka*

Casual gift, oh, gift unutile,
Life, why wert thou given me?
Why should Fate thus grant us futile
Terms of doomed mortality? . . .
—*Pushkin*

October 5, 1919
Motziv, Poland

Dear Tovah,

I thought we would be in America by now, but we remain in Poland, stranded by illness.

The sickness began with me. My legs and head started aching shortly after we crossed the Polish border.

I told Papa, "I am tired. That spray has made me sick."

By the time we arrived in Motziv my head pounded and my body hurt as if the train had run over me. I wanted only to rest. The motion of the train tormented me. I begged Papa for us to stop.

Mama and Papa took me off the train in Motziv. I did not know Papa had a cousin here, did you, Tovah? Papa's cousin did not have room for us, but he took us in anyway.

I don't remember very well what happened the first few weeks in Motziv. We slept on the floor in the shed of my father's cousin. I had dreams, terrible dreams about the guards at the train station and cossacks and entire forests chasing after me. Such nightmares!

I could not move at all. I felt imprisoned under a mound of stones.

I remember Papa down on the floor beside me, putting a damp cloth on my head. Papa is so good at nursing, but each time he placed the cloth over my eyes, I felt the weight of it crushing my head to the floor.

I tried to pull away from him, but whenever I moved, the pain exploded inside me. I begged Papa to stop, but the words would not come out. I could hardly draw breath, there was such a heaviness on my chest.

Saul says a student of medicine came to examine me. Papa had found a student to come who spoke Russian. By then a rash had crept under my armpits and across my back and my stomach. I had a cough that threatened to split me in two each time it erupted from me.

I had typhus.

The medical student said, "Her infection started in Russia. Someone she had contact with there gave this to her."

I wanted to tell this skinny, pock-faced man that he was wrong, that my illness did not come from Russia. I knew where it started. It came from the doctor at the Polish border. I tried to explain this to the man, but I could not speak.

"You must say nothing about the nature of her illness to anyone," the medical student told Papa. "Not even to your cousin. As for the child, she will probably die. Most do. That's how it goes with typhus."

I remember very little, Tovah, but I do remember that. Those words cut through the fever and the pain. When I heard them, I wished I could die. If I died, I would be free of my suffering.

But if I died, I would never reach America.

I remember Mama crying. I tried to speak, to say I would not die, that nothing would hold me back from America, but she couldn't hear me. No one could hear me.

"I should send you all back to Russia," the medical student said. "But the child would never survive the trip."

Papa begged him to let us stay. "I promise to care for her," he said.

The medical student agreed.

I lapsed into sleep on the floor in the miserable little shed while the typhus raged inside me.

Meanwhile, Mama and Papa and Nathan grew sick. They developed the typhus too. Only Saul managed to stay healthy. Saul is too much of an ox to get sick, Tovah.

Three men took Mama and Papa and Nathan in a cart to a hospital at the other end of Motziv.

I wept to see them go. I was still so sick, but I wept to see them. As they carried Papa out and loaded him into the cart beside Mama, I thought my life was over.

"Take me too!" I cried, but I had improved compared to Mama and Papa and Nathan.

"Motziv is full of typhus," the cart driver said. "We need the beds for the dying."

They left me with Saul, of all people. Saul, who never has a kind word for me. Saul, who pulls my hair and punches me, even though Mama says at sixteen he should know better.

Saul, with his big ears and his big feet, was all I had for a
nurse.

It is a wonder I did not die from the typhus. When Saul remembered, he held water to my lips so I could drink.

In my dreams and when I woke, I fretted over Mama and
Papa and Nathan. Were they already dead?

"Where is Mama?" I asked each time I woke from a restless
fever sleep. "Where is Papa?"

Saul turned his face away. He could not stand the smell of
me; I could tell by the way his mouth tightened. "Go back to
sleep, Rifka," he said. He always said the same. "Go back to
sleep."

Once I woke to find Saul kneeling beside me, holding my
hands down. His dark hair curled wildly around his ears. "What
are you doing to yourself?" he kept asking.

I had been dreaming about Mama's candlesticks. I was holding them against my chest. Hands, dozens of hands, reached
out of the darkness to take them from me. I tore at the hands,
trying to get them off me, trying to get them off Mama's candlesticks.

"Look what you've done to yourself," Saul said, touching the
tail of his shirt to my chest.

In my sleep, I had clawed at my chest until it bled.

Tovah, my hand is too weak to continue and my eyes blur at
these tiny letters, but I will write again soon.

Shalom,
Rifka

> A thirst in spirit, through the gloom
> Of an unpeopled waste I blundered . . .
> —*Pushkin*

November 3, 1919
Motziv, Poland

Dear Tovah,

I am doing much better now.

When I was well enough to move, Saul went out and found a new room for us to live in. "We cannot stay any longer in this shed," he said. Papa's family did not try to keep us from leaving. We had brought illness with us, and bad luck. We had taken from their table food they could not spare.

The room Saul found for us is in a cheap, rundown inn. The innkeeper hosts a large market outside his establishment every Wednesday. Merchants bring their wares and the innkeeper sells tea and rolls and buns. I think he makes a lot of money.

Market days are noisy. When my head aches, I cannot bear it. On my good days, though, I like to look out at the commotion.

Saul says the innkeeper is a thief, but we will stay here until Mama and Papa and Nathan are out of the hospital.

Saul found work to pay for our room and our food. He sorts apples in an orchard outside the village. At dawn, before leaving for work, Saul goes out to the street. He brings back breakfast for us, a herring and two rolls.

Each morning, when he comes with the food, Tovah, he splits it exactly in half. Even though he is bigger and needs more, he divides our food evenly.

Each day, we eat our herring and roll in a few bites and lick our fingertips to catch the crumbs. Then Saul leaves.

One day I took only a bite of my herring and decided to save the rest.

I told Saul I was not hungry.

It was a lie. I was hungry. I am hungry all the time. When I am awake, all I think about is food. When I sleep, I dream of it. My stomach twists and burns with emptiness.

But on this morning I thought, for once Saul is nice to me. I should be the same with him. Saul is working, he needs to eat more than I do. If I save my share of breakfast, it will be waiting for him in the evening when he returns.

I was still weak, but I knew I must get up and stow the herring and roll in the closet near my cot. If I did not put it away from myself, I would eat it.

My stomach knotted painfully, and in spite of my best intentions I took another bite of the herring before I closed the closet door. I hope you will not think I am too selfish, Tovah.

I turned my back on my precious food and tumbled into my cot, falling asleep immediately.

Movement in the room awakened me.

At first I thought Saul had come back, but it was not Saul. It was the girl whose father owns the inn. She sat on the edge of my cot, her thick, greasy braid hanging down her back.

She was eating something, herring and roll. The closet door was open. She was eating my herring and roll!

"Thief!" I cried in Russian. "Give me back my food!"

She ignored me. She sat on my cot, chewing.

I tried to get my roll back from her. She brushed me aside and laughed at me, Tovah.

She has so much food of her own. Always, when I see her passing by my room, she is chewing, her red cheeks swollen like a squirrel with a nut. The girl had spied on me. She had seen me save my food in the little closet and had come in and taken it for herself.

That family, they have rolls and buns all the time. It is the father's business. I drag myself from the drafty room Saul and I share and stand, swaying unsteadily in front of the bakery cases, staring at the innkeeper's food. I am so hungry, but no one offers me a crumb. The girl will be chewing, her tongue flicking out to catch a piece of bun and bring it back into her mouth again. She has all this food and she has to steal from me.

When Saul got back that evening, I told him about the girl stealing my food. I thought he would catch her and beat her up. Saul said, "Next time don't save your food, Rifka. Eat it. Then she can't take it from you."

And that was that.

With Saul gone all day, I felt lonely. Not that he was such good company, but I hated being alone, separated from Mama and Papa. In Berdichev, I could have gone to you, or to Aunt Anna, or to Bubbe Ruth.

But I was in a strange country, with no one to go to. I certainly would not go to the innkeeper's daughter, that dirty thief.

So when I grew strong enough, I started walking around Motziv. I found my way to the low, sprawling hospital where they were keeping Mama. I discovered a wooden ledge outside the window of Mama's ward and climbed on it to look in on her.

Mama lay in a narrow bed, as white as the sheet on top of her. Everything about Mama was white except her black hair. Her hair was like a dark stain on the hospital linens and her eyes remained closed, her thick lashes resting on white cheeks. She looked dead, Tovah, and I kept staring, waiting for her to move.

When the hospital workers caught me looking in at Mama, they yelled at me. They chased me away from the building. They couldn't understand that I needed to see Mama move. I needed to know she was alive. So the next day I came back, and the next day, and the next.

The Polish language has started making sense to me, Tovah. I didn't need to be clever to know I should stay out of the hospital workers' way, but I could not stay away from Mama.

Then, just this morning, a doctor caught me looking in at Mama. He did not chase me away. He lifted me down off the ledge.

"What are you doing here?" the doctor asked.

"I am watching over my mama," I explained.

The doctor asked, "Have you had the typhus?"

"Yes," I told him. "But I am better now."

The doctor said, "Come." He led me inside the hospital and sat me in a chair next to Mama's cot. "Once you have suffered through the typhus, you cannot have it again," the doctor explained. "It will do you no harm to sit with her. It may do her some good." I held Mama's hand and talked to her all the rest of today.

I even got to eat a potato out of the big pot brought by a lady who feeds the hospital patients.

They were good potatoes, Tovah. Since I have been sick, everything tastes good. How skinny I've become. But not Saul; he is as big as a horse. His legs have grown so long just since we left Russia. You should see how they sprout from his pants.

Even with all my things on, my underwear and my two extra dresses, and my cloak and shawl, I still do not look fat. Remember how in Berdichev the Russian guards would come to inspect the homes of the Jews? They made certain we owned no more than our allowance. Always, when the guards were coming, Mama would say, "Rifka, put all your clothes on." I would rush and throw my dresses over my head and stand out in front of the house to watch.

The guards would search through our rooms. They did not find more than two of anything. How could they find anything extra in our house? In your house there are many fine things, Tovah, but they never inspected your house.

The guards would look at me, layered in all my belongings, and say, "Hmmm, fat kid." With my dresses and my cloak and my shawl piled on top of me, I looked as short and round as a barrel.

I am no longer round, but I am still short. I wonder if I will ever grow, Tovah. Maybe it will be all right that I am short in America. If I could get Bubbe Ruth to come, there would at least be two of us.

If I could get Bubbe Ruth to come. She does not stay because she is comfortable and safe like you and Hannah and Uncle Avrum. Bubbe Ruth stays because she is afraid to leave, afraid for things to change. I am afraid too, but not so afraid that I want to come back.

I would like it best if you and Hannah and Uncle Avrum and Aunt Anna and Bubbe Ruth and all the others were coming to America too. I am trying to be clever, Tovah, but how much more clever I could be surrounded by my family.

> *Shalom, my cousin,*
> *Rifka*

… In hope, in torment, we are turning
Toward freedom, waiting her command …
—*Pushkin*

November 27, 1919
en route to Warsaw

Dear Tovah,

Many of the typhus patients at the hospital in Motziv died. We all survived. Now, at last, we are on our way to Warsaw. All of us—me, Mama, Papa, Nathan, and Saul.

Warsaw is where we pick up the money for our steamship tickets. My older brothers, Isaac and Reuben and Asher, have worked hard to save the money so we could join them in America. These other brothers of mine, they left Russia fourteen years ago, before my birth. Do *you* even remember them, Tovah?

They are my brothers, my family, but I don't know them. Papa showed me their letters. In my mind the letters came from strangers living in a distant land.

Then, only the day before we fled from Russia, the Red Cross posted the message on the board. Isaac and Reuben and Asher, they were sending for us. Remember how I ran to tell you our news? I wonder, Tovah, if the message still hangs there in the center of the village.

I am certain Warsaw is a wonderful city. When people in Motziv say the word "Warsaw," their voices deepen and they give a little kick on the end, like this: "Warsaw—ha!" It reminds me of the way we do in Berdichev when we speak of America.

Our train passes small herds of cattle grazing on yellowed grass and I remember the cows of Berdichev. The peasant girls drove them along the road past our house every night at sunset. Those cows were not bony as these are. I loved sitting on the front step watching the fat brown beasts lumber past. The earth shivered beneath their clopping weight as the sun set in a ball of fire. Those girls sang in such beautiful harmony.

When I read your Pushkin, I remember those cows, and the girls' singing.

Poland is so cold and flat and colorless. Only pine trees, scrubby, wretched pine trees, sweep past the window of the train. Maybe in the spring it is better, maybe there are flowers. Maybe the sky is something other than gray. Now, it is nearly December, and I shiver at the cold of Poland.

It is odd to see Mama and Papa and Nathan so changed. In Berdichev, Mama kept us all well on practically nothing. You know what a baker she is. Always the smell of yeast clung to her.

Many times she would send me to your house with a basket of pastries or a cake, or her thick dark bread. There is no baking for her now.

Papa's dark eyes have lost their spark since the typhus, and Mama's long black hair does not shine as it once did. Even Nathan, with his thick black curls and his strong dimpled jaw, has hollowed cheeks and circles beneath his eyes. I cannot tell how I look, but Mama sometimes strokes my cheek and sighs. Her fingers are bony and rough.

Only Saul still glows with health from his clumsy feet to his big red ears.

I must tell you of this noisy, crowded, stinking train we are riding north out of Motziv. The freight train from Berdichev was more comfortable. Here people push against one another on every bench. The cars are drafty and reek of old bedding. Between the chugging and the clacking tracks and the endless Polish babble, the noise never stops pressing against you. Worse still, there is no place to relieve yourself and I drank two cups of tea before we boarded. I could not sit still a moment longer.

"I am going for a walk," I told Mama.

Mama nodded, still chewing slowly her lunch of cold potato and roll. I had finished the last bite of mine long ago.

At the back of our car a peasant girl sat on a bench with a baby sucking at her breast. At first I thought the girl was older, but when she looked up, I saw she was your age, Tovah, near sixteen.

Her blond hair hung thinly down from her kerchief, tickling the baby's bald head. The baby's fingers played on the girl's cheek as it nursed.

The girl noticed me staring. "You like babies?" she asked in Polish, talking over the heads of the passengers beside her.

I nodded and fiddled with the knot of my kerchief.

"You have beautiful hair," she said. "Mine . . ." She took her free hand and flipped the wisps of hair over her shoulder. "My sister used to fix my hair. Until she married and moved away. I am going to visit her now, my sister."

I do not know what made me offer. Maybe it was the sweetness of the baby, maybe the friendliness of the girl. "I used to fix my cousin's hair," I said in Polish. "I could fix yours so you will look nice for your sister . . . if you'd like."

She was happy to let me fix her hair. I pushed into the narrow space between the bench and the back of the train car and removed her kerchief.

Her head stank. Strands of hair clustered in oily clumps. Most terrible, though, were big round sores all over her scalp.

My fingers hesitated. I did not wish to touch the girl's head, yet neither did I wish to insult her. I gathered the ends of her hair and began unknotting the tangles.

Tilting her head back, the girl sighed as I worked my fingers through the snarls.

The baby pulled its mouth off the girl's breast and looked up at me. Its mouth opened into a milky smile.

"You have a nice baby," I said.

The girl turned and looked me over. "You are not Polish."

I was afraid everyone on the train heard her. I worried they'd send me back to Berdichev as the Polish border guards had threatened, or that they'd chase me away as the nurses did in Motziv. To my relief, the other passengers ignored us and the girl turned back around.

"I am from Ukraine," I whispered. "I am going with my family to America."

"America!" the girl said. "America."

The man sitting beside her inched away, forcing an old woman on the end of the bench to plant her feet firmly on the floor to keep from falling.

"America," the girl repeated. "What will you do there?"

I was silent for a little time.

"I will do everything there," I answered.

The girl threw back her head and laughed. Standing over her, I saw that several of her teeth were missing.

She said, "Why would you want to go to America? You can do everything you want right here. I would never leave Poland."

"Never?" I asked.

"I can't imagine going out my door and finding anything else. Look at it out there. That is home."

I looked out the train window. There was a boy running across a frozen field with a black dog loping along at his side. For a moment I saw Poland as she saw it.

Then my eyes saw the bleakness outside the window again and I felt a chill creep down my spine.

"There," I said, smoothing out the last tangle from her hair and backing away shyly. "I must return to my family."

She put a finger to her lips, revealing a cracked and reddened nail. Her baby slept with its little nose squashed against her breast.

"Good luck to you in America," she whispered.

I stumbled back up the aisle of the lurching train, thrown against this one's shoulder, squeezing past that one. The smell of cheese filled the car. My mouth watered at the stench of it.

I slid back into my place between Mama and Nathan and looked around at the other people in the car, listening to their conversations.

I felt your Pushkin inside my rucksack and I wanted to get it out and write my thoughts. I am filling the pages of our book quickly, Tovah, even with my writing so small and fine.

"Mama?" I asked, feeling her elbow rub against my ribs with the motion of the train. "Can I get off for a little while at the next station? The stops are so long. Could I get off just for a moment?"

"No."

"But Mama, I have to go . . ."

"No," Mama said. "I told you not to drink that tea this morning."

"I'm bored, Mama," I said.

I was afraid to tell her the truth, Tovah. To tell her I wanted only to find a quiet corner, where I could open our Pushkin. She did not like your teaching me Pushkin in Berdichev. If Mama had her way, I would know how to cook, and sew, and keep the Sabbath. That is all.

"You are bored?" Mama said. "So I'll hire you a band. You are not getting off this train, Rifka. What if it left without you? You want we should get separated? You want to spend the rest of your life in Poland? No, Rifka, you stay right where you are. Here I can keep an eye on you. Here you are safe."

So I kept my thoughts in my head until this moment. Mama and Saul snore softly at the end of the bench. Papa and Nathan have gone off to stretch their long legs.

As I write, I am thinking that sometimes I don't like growing up, Tovah. Sometimes I wish I could run back to Berdichev, into Bubbe Ruth's arms, and lose myself inside her warmth. She protected me from everything around me and inside me.

But then at other times I am so glad to be who I am. Rifka Nebrot. Only daughter and youngest child of Ethel and Beryl

Nebrot. Baby sister of Isaac and Asher and Reuben and Nathan and Saul. Traveling forward—to America.

When I think of myself that way, even though we are homeless and our lives are in danger even now, still I believe everything will turn out well.

Shalom, my cousin,
Rifka

. . . Goal, there can be none before me,
Empty-hearted, idle-willed.
Life's monotony rolls o'er me,
Tired with longings unfulfilled.

—*Pushkin*

November 30, 1919
Warsaw, Poland

Dear Tovah,

What should I do? I hold the worst news in my heart. Whatever shall I do?

As soon as we finished our business at the bank in Warsaw, we followed directions to the steamship office. How rich we felt with all the money my brothers had sent us from America. How eager we were to start our journey across the ocean.

Before they sell you your ticket, though, Tovah, you must have an examination by a doctor.

I think doctors are the cruelest men upon this earth. This doctor, who worked for the steamship company, took me and Mama into a room. He examined us for deformities and disease.

He examined our bodies and our eyes.

"Take off your kerchiefs," he said. "I will check your scalps."

My head had been itching terribly for the past day. I gladly removed my kerchief and gave my head a good scratching.

The doctor washed his hands after he examined me.

"Mrs. Nebrot," he told my mother, "you have passed your examination. You may go now to buy your ticket."

"Come along, Rifka," Mama said, gathering her belongings.

"No," the doctor said. "I am sorry. Your daughter cannot join you. Our company will not sell her passage to America."

Mama said, "You don't understand. She must go to America."

"She can't," the doctor answered. "She has a skin disease, ringworm. You see these sores on her scalp?" I thought of the Polish girl on the train, the girl with the baby. She had sores on her scalp.

Mama's dark eyes widened. "Rifka, Rifka," she murmured. Her hands shook. "How do we get rid of this—this ringworm?"

"There is a treatment," the doctor said. "But it takes many months."

All of me went numb. Only my heart beat thickly in my chest.

Before he showed us out of his room, the doctor wrote something on a piece of paper. He handed it to Mama and told her to give the paper to the man at the steamship office window.

Papa tried bribing the steamship officials. It is a trick he learned in Berdichev from your father, a trick where money put in the right pocket can get you almost anything.

"Here," Papa said to the man in the steamship office, pushing our precious money into his hand. "Please, take this to make my daughter Rifka a ticket."

The man looked at Papa's money. He looked at the five of us standing before him. "Wait here," he said.

He went to the other room, the room where the doctor sat. He came back shortly.

"I'm sorry," he said, returning to his post at the window.

"Is it not enough?" Papa asked, reaching into his pockets. "You need to have more?"

"No more," the man said. "What you ask is impossible. The child cannot go."

"Why can't I go?" I demanded.

The man paid no attention to me. He spoke to Mama and Papa. "If the child arrives in America with this disease, the Americans will turn her around and send her right back to Poland. My company will have to pay the cost of her return. If my company has to do this for your daughter, the doctor and I will no longer have our jobs. I'm sorry. There's nothing I can do."

Tovah! I can't go to America! They will let Mama and Papa and Saul and Nathan go. But they won't let me. I cannot stay here in Warsaw without Mama and Papa! How can I live without Mama and Papa to care for me, to protect me?

Yesterday Mama gave me a handful of money and sent me outside to wait for her and Papa.

"You stay out of trouble," Mama said. "We'll try our luck at *this* steamship company; perhaps they will not mind about your ringworm."

Outside, a bony old man with a nose like a parsnip sat with a basket at his feet full of round orange fruit. I stared at him and stared at him. Finally I went over.

"What is this?" I asked in Polish, pointing to the fruit. From a distance, I had seen a similar fruit in Motziv at the market outside our inn. That fruit was small, more yellow than orange, with patches of green. These were perfect autumn-colored balls.

"Oranges," the old man answered. He had no teeth in his mouth.

"How much for one?" I asked, inhaling the bright smell of fruit wafting up from his basket. My stomach grumbled eagerly and my mouth grew wet.

"How much you have?" he asked. When he spoke, bits of spittle stretched between his lips. He stared straight at me. I was not being clever then, Tovah. I held out my handful of money. He took it all and handed me one orange.

A few moments later, Mama came out and saw me biting through the bitter skin of the fruit. "Where did you get that?" she asked. "Where is the money I gave you, Rifka?"

I took her to the old man, but the man cried, "There you are! Thief! You steal my oranges! Help! Police! What monster are you, to steal from an old man!"

"I did not!" I cried. "I paid you. You took all the money I had!"

"Liar!" the old man screamed. "Liar and thief!" His spittle flew through the air. A drop landed on the back of my hand. I rubbed and rubbed it against my coat but I could not get the feel of it off me. Finally Papa gave him more money to quiet him.

I lost our food money, Tovah. Mama yelled at me and Saul made a horrible face. I bit my lip to keep from crying. The taste of the orange still danced in my mouth. I will never eat another orange as long as I live!

Mama said, "What will we do? We have to eat."

"Hush," Papa said. "I will think of something."

"It is not your fault, Rifka," Nathan whispered. He tried smiling, but his dimples barely showed.

Now we have no money for food. Tovah, I think there is no hope I will ever be clever.

That tells you about Warsaw. How can Mama and Papa leave me in such a city?

Warsaw is bigger than any city I have ever seen. The buildings are so tall, I get dizzy looking up at them. There are carriages that move without horses to pull them. They are called "cars," and they prowl the streets like frenzied wolves.

Warsaw is a horrible place, Tovah. I can never stay here.

> *Pray for me, please,*
> *Rifka*

> . . . As conquered by the last cold air,
> When winter whistles in the wind,
> Alone upon a branch that's bare
> A trembling leaf is left behind.
>
> —*Pushkin*

December 1, 1919
Warsaw, Poland

Dear Tovah,

Papa and Mama met with a lady from the HIAS. That is the Hebrew Immigrant Aid Society. They are a group of people who help Jews with troubles like ours. The lady said the HIAS has workers all over the world. I wonder why we never met any in Berdichev or Motziv. Have you heard of them?

The lady from the HIAS gave us money to buy food. She sat with us in our room and listened to our troubles. She was no taller than I am. Wisps of silver hair kept escaping from a bun on the top of her head.

She said, "Mr. and Mrs. Nebrot, you and your two sons should leave for America as planned. But, Rifka must stay until her ringworm heals."

"To leave a child of twelve?" Papa said. "How can we do such a thing?"

"It is not so unusual," the HIAS lady said. "We have handled many such cases."

Awful things are happening to me, Tovah. My hair is falling out, my long blond hair. I have a bald patch over one ear and another on the back of my head. I can cover it with the kerchief, but it itches and itches. I know I must be ugly because Mama's eyes look away from me all the time now.

"Can't Mama stay with me?" I asked.

The lady from the HIAS said, "If your mama goes to America, she can work and make money for the family. She can make a home for your father and your brothers. If your mama stays in Europe with you, she will cost the family money. Only you must stay, Rifka."

"I will not stay in Warsaw," I told the lady from the HIAS. "If my family leaves me in Warsaw, I will find a way back to my home in Berdichev."

The lady from the HIAS said, "I want you to leave Warsaw also, but not for Berdichev. The cure for your illness awaits you in Belgium."

Mama said, "Belgium? What is Belgium? I have never heard of this place."

"It is the best place for Rifka now," the HIAS lady said. "The people of Belgium open their arms and their homes to immigrants."

That is what I am, Tovah. That is what you are when you are wandering between two worlds. You are an immigrant.

The HIAS lady said, "We can arrange for Rifka to stay with a family in Antwerp. She will go each day to a hospital and get treatment for her ringworm. When you are all better, Rifka, you can sail to America right from Antwerp and join your mama and papa and all your brothers."

"I don't want to stay with a family I don't know," I said. I remembered the innkeeper's daughter in Motziv, the one who ate my herring. What if the family I stay with in Belgium is like hers?

I do not want to be anywhere without my family. Even Saul would be better than no one. If they would just let Saul stay with me.

Saul does not want to stay. All Saul cares about is getting to America.

The HIAS lady said, "In Antwerp there will be someone from my organization to look out for you, to monitor your care."

I said, "If I can't go to America, please send me back to Berdichev."

Papa said, "Rifka, the Russians are angry at our family in Berdichev. We have cheated them of five strong boys. The army wanted your brothers, they wanted Isaac and Asher and Reuben and Nathan and Saul. I could not let them have my sons."

Nathan sat with his hands clasped in his lap. Saul stood with his back to me, staring out the little window of our room.

"Rifka," Papa said, "you cannot go back to our home in Berdichev. We have no more home in Berdichev. You, too, would meet your death if you returned now. Your coming back would put all the family remaining, Tovah and Bubbe Ruth and Aunt Anna and all the others, in greater danger."

I don't want to put you in danger, Tovah. I must go to Belgium, I see that, but I feel so frightened. What will become of me?

Tovah, I am like an orphan now.

> *Shalom,*
> *Rifka*

> . . . Sleep evades me, there's no light:
> Darkness wraps the earth with slumber,
> Only weary tickings number
> The slow hours of the night. . . .
>
> —*Pushkin*

February 25, 1920
Antwerp, Belgium

Dear Tovah,

Saying good-bye to Mama and Papa hurt in my chest the way it hurt when Saul held me underwater too long. The night before, Mama had slipped off her gold locket. I had never seen Mama without her locket. It came from Papa, his wedding gift to her. Mama hung the gold chain around my neck. I wrapped my hand around it and felt Mama's warmth in the etched metal.

Papa gave me his tallis, his precious prayer shawl. He said a prayer over it first, kissed the fringe, then handed it to me.

"Why should she have Papa's tallis?" Saul muttered. "She is only a girl."

"Hush, Saul," Nathan said. "Don't make things worse."

The HIAS lady in Warsaw put me on my train the same day Mama, Papa, Nathan, and Saul left. I waved good-bye to them until my arm ached, but too soon, crowds pushed between us, and they were gone.

My train took me through Germany and into Belgium. So now I am in Antwerp. It has taken me a little while to get settled. The first room the Hebrew Immigrant Aid Society found for me was dark and stuffy, like the inside of your wardrobe, Tovah. Now I am in a very nice room.

The couple who own this house are older even than Mama and Papa. They tell me to call them Gaston and Marie. Can you imagine, Tovah? They have very nice things. A quilt of blue squares covers my bed and a little red desk sits under the window. I sit at the desk for hours, fitting perfectly because I am so short, and I look out the window at the park below or read our Pushkin. I have a pitcher and bowl decorated with tiny blue flowers and a chest to keep my clothes in.

There is a painting on the wall over my bed. It shows a countryside covered with wildflowers. When I look at it, I think this is what it is like in America.

I have a braided rug to warm my feet. The woman, Marie, made it herself. She has made many of the things here.

This is the nicest place I have ever lived. My room is almost as fine as the rooms in your house, Tovah.

But it is not home. It can never be home without Mama and Papa. I miss them so much.

Papa wrote that they have settled in New York City. His letters tell about their trip across the ocean and their apartment. They have water right outside their door and a real indoor toilet just down the hall. It is odd to think of Mama and Papa living in such luxury.

My thirteenth birthday came last week. I did not tell Marie and Gaston.

I had hoped to celebrate this birthday in America.

I remember my ninth birthday when you and Hannah gave me the doll. What a beautiful doll she was, with a china head. Every morning I would smear her face with herring, pretending she was eating breakfast too.

Mama and Saul took that doll. I remember how they took her, along with the dress Aunt Rachel had made for me. I could never tell you this. Papa forbade us to speak to anyone about such matters. But Mama and Saul took my doll and my dress and traded them at the market for potatoes. I swore I would not eat those potatoes, but I got hungry and I ate.

In America, no one will take my gifts from me.

So I am thirteen now. For Nathan and Saul's thirteenth birthdays, Mama and Papa made a mitzvah. I am just a girl. Still, girl or not, I think God would want me to have a mitzvah too.

Early on the morning of my birthday, I crept down the stairs and took broken straws from the kitchen broom.

Back in my room, I wove the straws into a Star of David, a fragile golden Star of David. It took patience and time to twine the straws so they would hold together. When I finished, I set my star on the red desk beside Mama's locket and the sunlight fell on them both. I stood before the window, wrapped in Papa's tallis, and recited all the Hebrew prayers I held in my memory. Maybe you would think me foolish, Tovah, but I made a mitzvah. I celebrated my becoming a woman, just like the boys do when they become men.

Later, I placed my Star of David between the pages of our Pushkin, so I could keep it forever to remember this day.

Before I went to sleep that night, I read over my letters to you.
I ran out of blank pages in the book a long time ago. Now I write
in the margins around the poetry. Someday I will get these letters to you, Tovah. I promise. When I reach America, Papa will
show me how to send this properly and you will have your
Pushkin back again. In America, I can buy my own Pushkin . . .
and any other book I wish to read.

My hair is gone. All gone. I am as bald as the rabbi of Berdichev.
I cover my baldness with a kerchief, but still I look very ugly.

I don't ever leave my room. It is winter. Back in our village, I
was always first out to skate on the pond. In Antwerp, I do not
go outside, except for my treatments.

The treatments are not so bad as I feared. I walk to the convent
once a day. The nun in charge of my case is Sister Katrina. She
washes my scalp with a green soap that makes my eyes water.
Then she puts me under a violet light. The light warms my head.

"You don't mind the treatments, do you, Rifka?" Sister
Katrina asks.

I smile and shake my head. I do not mind. In Belgium, where
I am neither held nor loved, it feels good when Sister Katrina
touches me, even if she does so only to treat my ringworm.

When my scalp is perfectly dry, Sister Katrina sprinkles it
with powder. She gave me two new kerchiefs, pretty ones. She
boils and dries them each time before I can wear them.

"Cleanliness is important in curing your disease," Sister
Katrina says.

She also makes me clean my nails. "You can make the disease worse by scratching the sores with your fingers," she says.

I tell her, "My nails are clean. See!"

She says, "You can't see the germs that make the ringworm,
Rifka. Here, scrub your nails."

So I do.

I don't scratch my head that much anyway. Just sometimes I
can't help it. Sister Katrina is teaching me Flemish. She taught
me a prayer to say in my head when I need to scratch. I think
saying the prayer is supposed to keep my mind off the itching. I
am not sure it is right, though, for a Jew to say Catholic prayers.
I say a Hebrew prayer instead.

The sister is nice. She has dimples even deeper than Nathan's:
so deep, I can see them even when she is not smiling. Papa
sends me money in his letters. He writes that I must pay Sister
Katrina for the care she gives me.

I count out the money they send. I think Mama and Papa

must be getting rich in America, working in the clothing factory. I think soon they will be as rich as Uncle Avrum.

Then I worry that maybe they are going without food to send this money to me.

Sister Katrina accepts nothing. "Keep it," she says. "You need it more."

She talks with me during my treatment. At first we spoke only in Polish, but I am picking up Flemish quickly.

After my treatments she makes tea. Sister Katrina tells me I am clever because I learn Flemish so easily. I thought you would like that, Tovah, that someone thinks I am clever.

"Really it is not so clever," I tell her. "It is nothing special. I just learn these things."

"You will learn even faster if you get out of your room," Sister Katrina says. "Antwerp is a lovely city. Go out, enjoy yourself."

"I like my room," I say. "It too is lovely. I am happy to stay there." I can't explain to her how I fear this city filled with strangers.

"You do not get enough exercise," Sister Katrina says. "You go from your room to the convent and back again. Explore more. Go on. It won't hurt you. What you need, Rifka, is some fresh Belgian air."

It is not exercise and fresh air I need. It is Mama and Papa. How can I enjoy myself without Mama, without my family? I do not need exercise. All I need is to get better and to go to America.

Walking to and from the convent, I pass many beautiful sights. There are gardens everywhere, and even in the winter I can see how fine they are. I pass a market filled with fruits and vegetables and buckets of flowers of every color. And smells that make my stomach always eager to eat.

Right now I am sitting at the little desk in my room, looking out over the park. There are children who come every day. I'm beginning to recognize them. There is one girl, built so much like Hannah, slender with dark eyes and dark hair. Once or twice I have almost gone out only to be near her.

I would like to play with her, to play with all of them, but what if it is like Russia and they hate me because I am a Jew? What if it is like Poland and they hate me because I am not a Pole? What if they hate me because I have no hair?

I wish I could be back with you, Tovah, and with Hannah. Remember how Hannah would dress me up and coil my hair around her fingers? When I grew sleepy, she would set me on the warm shelf of the tiled stove and cover me in furs and sing to me.

And you. You would talk, always talk.

"Listen to this, Rifka," you would say, and you would read me something from one of Uncle Avrum's big books. Or you would open the Pushkin and sometimes your voice would go deep and husky. I could not understand why, but tears would stand in both our eyes. Tovah, I loved the words that sprang from your lips. It is you, my cousin, who made me want to learn.

Hannah is like a fairy princess, so delicate and beautiful and sweet. You, Tovah, are like an old rabbi, clever and funny and brave.

Is Hannah still taking piano lessons? Marie plays piano. She is playing now.

Don't tell this to Hannah, but I used to hate listening to her lessons. The teacher would scream and tears would roll down Hannah's cheeks. She never got the notes right.

It is you who can really play, Tovah, and never a lesson of your own. It amazed me how you could watch Hannah's lesson and then sit down after and play the music yourself. I never understood why Uncle Avrum didn't give you lessons.

When I asked Mama, she said, "Uncle Avrum won't give Tovah piano lessons because of her back."

"Well," I told Mama, "just because Tovah's back isn't straight doesn't mean she can't play the piano. When she was a baby and fell from the table did she hurt anything else? Did she hurt her hands so she couldn't play? No! So why can't Tovah have piano lessons?"

Mama said, "You couldn't understand, Rifka."

"I can," I insisted. "Explain to me."

Mama said, "Uncle Avrum gives Hannah piano lessons so she can catch a good husband."

"What about Tovah?" I asked. "Doesn't Uncle Avrum want her to catch a good husband too?"

Mama said, "Some girls aren't meant to marry, Rifka."

"But Tovah is smart and funny!" I cried. "And so clever . . ." I thought everyone saw you as I did.

Now that I am bald, I wonder. Maybe Mama would think I am one of those girls too. One of those girls not meant to marry.

Sister Katrina says my hair will grow back. What if it doesn't? I think you would still love me, just as I love you. Bubbe Ruth, my dear little grandmother, she would love me, even with a bald head. But you are both very far away.

My own mama watched with such sorrow my hair falling out, and she left before it was done. What would she think if she saw me now? I have started praying for my hair to grow back.

Sometimes I even say Sister Katrina's prayer, even if it is for Catholics. I hope that does not make things worse for me.

> *Shalom, dear Tovah,*
> *Rifka*

With freedom's seed the desert sowing,
I walked before the morning star . . .
—*Pushkin*

March 17, 1920
Antwerp, Belgium

Dear Tovah,

Today I have met Antwerp. Even though it is still winter, the air blew soft and mild today. All along my walk back from the convent, windows were open. Sounds from the houses drifted out into the street.

I took a different route home, turning down one new lane, then another and another. I passed millineries and bakeries and big department stores. I passed barbers and markets and tailor shops.

I came to a café with heavy wooden doors flung wide open. Big green flowerpots sat on either side of the doorway and a wild strange music streamed out from the dark room. Most amazing of all, a giant man stood there, filling the doorway of the café. I had never seen such a man before. I thought my papa and my brothers were big, but they were nothing beside this man.

I must have been staring.

The giant looked down at me. He grinned—a grin so wide it was like the entrance to a tunnel. Inside that enormous mouth were teeth of pure gold!

I know you will not think this very clever of me, Tovah, but when I saw all those shining teeth in his huge dark mouth I was afraid. I turned and started running. I ran and ran until I could run no more. Leaning back against a low brick wall, I gasped for breath.

I didn't recognize anything.

I tried to find my way back, but I couldn't.

The sun began to set and the warmth of the day vanished. A brisk wind blew through the streets, up the alleys, across the canals. I had not enough clothes on. I tried to keep myself from shaking, but the twilight chilled me. I was lost. I did not have the least idea how to get back to the house on King Street.

A milkman steered his horse and cart up the narrow street in the twilight. The cart clinked softly with empty bottles. I followed him, remembering Uncle Zeb and his horse, Lotkeh, and how

Uncle Zeb would take me for rides when he didn't have business.

I did not know what this milkman would do to me if I stopped him. Uncle Zeb would have helped a lost child. But in Berdichev, if a Jew stopped the wrong person, they might end up dead.

I am not in Berdichev, I told myself. I am in Antwerp, and Sister Katrina and the lady from the HIAS have told me not to fear the people of Antwerp.

Well, I thought, if I am to make it back to my room tonight, I had better ask someone. So I called to the milkman sitting tall on his cart.

"Please," I asked. "Can you show me the way to King Street?"

He was tall and thin. He had a black mustache that hid his mouth altogether.

"Please," I said again, beginning in Flemish, finishing in Yiddish. "I am very . . . lost."

As he climbed down out of his cart he smiled at me. I could tell he smiled by the way his mustache lifted around his chin.

He took my face in his long fingers and smiled down at me.

"King Street?" he asked. "Come." The milkman clicked softly to his horse.

"My uncle drove a cart," I said, jabbering nervously as he walked me through the streets of Antwerp. "His horse's name was Lotkeh. I don't know where Lotkeh is anymore. Bubbe Ruth sold him after my uncle's death."

The milkman led his horse with one hand. He offered me his other. I hesitated for a moment, then took it.

"My uncle used to take me for rides in his cart when he had no customers," I chattered in a mixture of Flemish and Yiddish, gripping the milkman's hand tightly. "Not that I don't like walking. I don't mind walking at all."

The milkman nodded, even though he could not understand all I said to him.

"It is very nice of you to help me," I said. "My uncle was nice too. I think maybe you are a lot like him. My uncle was a very patient man."

The milkman glanced down at me. His mustache hairs tickled his bottom lip. His eyes were two warm coals in his long face. It felt good to be talking to him, holding his hand like I would hold Papa's, or Uncle Avrum's, or Uncle Zeb's.

The milkman not only took me back to King Street, which I can only think was well out of his way. He took me to my very own door on King Street.

Tovah, he did not look like Uncle Zeb, except for the kindness in his eyes, but still, while I was with him, I felt Uncle Zeb near me. Outside the door of my house in Antwerp, the milkman bowed to me in parting.

I would not let go of his hand. There were hairs along the back of it, stiff dark hairs. I do not know why, Tovah, but I took that long hand of the milkman and pressed it to my lips. I kissed the strong, leathery hand of the milkman, right out in front of the house on King Street.

I never had a chance to say good-bye to Uncle Zeb. The soldiers shot him as he came out of his house. That was that. Kissing the hand of the milkman, I felt at last I could say good-bye to Uncle Zeb too.

The milkman bowed to me once again. Then he lifted his long legs into his cart and he drove away.

It is late now. My candle burns low. I wonder, Tovah. How do you thank people for such kindness? I never knew strangers could be so kind. Do you think my brothers Asher and Reuben and Isaac would have done as much? I hope so.

Shalom, my dear cousin,
Rifka

> . . . And I shall know some savor of elation
> Amidst the cares, the woes, and the vexation . . .
>
> —*Pushkin*

July 29, 1920
Antwerp, Belgium

Dear Tovah,

Antwerp is a wonderful city. The people are so kind and generous, even the children.

I play with them in the park outside my room. Gizelle is the name of the girl who reminds me of Hannah. She really isn't like Hannah at all, now that I've come to know her. She is more practical and solid than Hannah. She brings her ball to the park and we play catch. I have learned many bouncing rhymes though I don't always understand what I am singing. The children laugh at my accent, but not in a cruel way.

It seems I have lived in Antwerp always. The old couple I board with, Marie and Gaston, are kind to me. They enjoy when I speak with them in Flemish. Gaston laughs and claps his hands when I tell him a story about my day. "Listen to her, Marie," he crows. "Is she not wonderful?"

I can hardly believe that it ever felt strange to me here. The bridges over the canals, the market at the Grunaplatz, the beautiful carriages and horses trotting along the streets, the cabarets and the hula dancers, they are all so familiar to me now. I wish Mama and Papa were here. The boys, too. And you, Tovah, and Hannah and Uncle Avrum and Bubbe Ruth, everyone, I wish you were all here. How I would love to share this wonderful city with you.

Not only are the people kind in Belgium, but the food is splendid. Sister Katrina and the lady from the HIAS have introduced me to so many new tastes. Almost always, I eat in the market. It costs very little, so I am saving Papa's money, and the food, Tovah, you wouldn't believe. There is a fruit called a banana, colored yellow like a June sun and curved. You peel the skin off and underneath is a white fruit so sweet and creamy, it makes even Frusileh's milk seem thin by comparison.

And ice cream! If the people in Berdichev could taste ice cream, they would give up eating everything else. In the afternoon, the ice cream man comes down King Street with a giant dog pulling his cart.

He rings a little bell as he walks and we crowd around him. The dog wags its tail and stands very still. I never knew such a dog and such a man.

And there is chocolate. This food I found without anyone's help. Belgian chocolate. It is like biting off a little corner of heaven—even better than Mama's pastry, may she never hear me say that.

I told Sister Katrina how much I like the chocolate. Now she always has a piece for me to eat with the tea she serves after my treatment.

"You must eat foods that are good for you, too, Rifka," she says. "Not just chocolate."

"I know," I answer, but often I eat nothing but ice cream, and chocolate, and bananas. See, Tovah, I am a little clever. I have found one advantage to being on my own. I eat exactly as I please.

Sister Katrina says the ringworm is beginning to heal. She is happy with my progress, but I can tell she worries that there is no hair yet.

In Antwerp, it doesn't seem to matter that I have no hair. When I first arrived, the lady from the HIAS took me shopping. She took me to a department store and helped me choose some dresses.

I needed new clothes. The Belgians fumigate all your belongings before they let you enter their country, just as the Polish do. Of course the Belgians are far more kind in the way they treat you. But after two fumigations, my old clothes were falling to pieces.

While I was shopping with the lady from the HIAS that first week, I saw a hat that I wanted, a hat that would cover my baldness. I thought if I only owned such a hat, it would not matter so much that I was bald . . . but I did not have the money.

So I started saving, and as soon as I could, I returned to the department store. I would have that hat. With that hat I would not be ashamed of the way I look. With that hat I could hold my head up anywhere. But when I got to the store, the hat was gone. Sold to someone else.

"We can make you another," said the salesclerk. She took my measurements without saying a word about the scabs on my head. A new hat was made, just for me.

It is black velvet with shirring. The brim has light blue velvet underneath. Now that the ringworm is clearing up, I don't have to wear kerchiefs all the time. I don't have to sterilize every stitch of cloth that comes near my head. I don't have to look like a poor, needy immigrant Jew from Berdichev.

I'm hoping I can go to America soon. Sometimes I think I will lose my mind longing for Mama, her yeasty hands, her red-cheeked face. And Papa, wrapped in his tallis, davening, his knees bent slightly, his body bobbing forward and back, praying in the gray light of dawn. I ache to smell the kindled Sabbath candles and to hear Papa and Mama's voices raised in prayer. Just to hold them and be held by them once more. I miss them so much. And the way Nathan brushed my hair. How he smoothed my tangled curls more gently than Mama ever did. I miss even Saul, and his big feet and his teasing.

I wonder if I can learn to make ice cream when I get to America. I know it has something to do with the milk from a cow. Maybe Bubbe Ruth and Frusileh can go into business. The Russians don't forbid Jews to make ice cream, yet. At least not that I know. Maybe Bubbe Ruth can earn enough money making ice cream; she can be as well-to-do as you and Hannah and Uncle Avrum.

If I can't get you and Bubbe out of the Old World, maybe I can at least give to you something from the new.

> *Shalom, my cousin,*
> *Rifka*

... The sister of misfortune, Hope,
In the under-darkness dumb
Speaks joyful courage to your heart:
The day desired will come. ...
— *Pushkin*

September 14, 1920
Antwerp, Belgium

Dear Tovah,

I am going to America! The nun, Sister Katrina, says my ringworm is completely cured, and the doctor signed my papers.
"Godspeed," he said. "Go ahead."

At last I am free to go to America, to join Mama and Papa and
all my giant brothers. It has been an entire year since leaving
Berdichev. Such a year!

My hair still has not started growing. Sister Katrina says perhaps it never will. I can't imagine going through life with no hair
on my head. There are wigs, perukes, but a short, ugly peruke
on my head? What a thought!

My hair was the only nice thing about me. Still, I am trying to
remember your advice, Tovah, to rely on my wits and not my
looks. I don't look so bad in a hat or with my kerchief, not really,
once you get used to it. I hope Mama can get used to it. As for
my being clever ... even with what Sister Katrina and the lady
from the HIAS say about me and languages, I'm still not so sure.

The lady from the HIAS helped me to buy my ticket. She
looks very much like the HIAS lady in Warsaw: little and ener-
getic, with an unruly silver bun on top of her head. Maybe they
must all look like this to work for the HIAS. Maybe I should also
work for the HIAS when I grow up. I am certainly the right
height. Though I might have difficulty with the bun if my hair
does not grow.

The HIAS lady took me around to the steamship company as
soon as the doctor gave me permission to leave. She advised me
to buy a ticket on a small ship leaving Antwerp tomorrow. I
could wait for two more weeks and sail on a big ship, but I don't
want to wait. Besides, if I sailed on the big ship, I would have to

sail to America in steerage. Steerage is what they call it when all the poor people crowd together down in the belly of the ship. People in steerage have no privacy, not an inch of space to turn from their left to their right. That is how Mama and Papa went across the ocean, and from the way they described it in their letter, I wouldn't like it very much at all. The rich people on such boats travel in first class or second class, but the poor people travel in steerage.

So I bought my ticket on a ship that has no classes. All the people traveling to America on this ship are equal. It is very democratic. "Democratic" is one of the words the lady from the HIAS has taught me.

I have been learning English. The HIAS lady brings me books and tutors me. Once she took me to an American movie about Tom Mix. Tom Mix is a cowboy, Tovah. Do you know what that is? He rides around on a horse all the time and shoots at bad people. I think Tom Mix loves his horse as much as Uncle Zeb loved Lotkeh.

I remember Uncle Zeb now like he was in a dream. So many new things fill my life, Tovah. I need to remind myself of how we struggled in Berdichev.

If it were not for the Pushkin, and for these letters to you, I would sometimes think I had dreamed all the terrible things about Russia. But when I read the Pushkin, I know my memories are real.

This morning I said good-bye to my friends in the park, especially Gizelle. I have decided to bring a present to Sister Katrina, to thank her for all she has done. She loves flowers. I will go to the market at the Grunaplatz and buy her the most beautiful bouquet I can find. I have money. Papa has been sending it to me all along, and except for some food and clothes, I have spent very little. Tonight, Marie and Gaston have planned for me a little party.

Tovah, when I get to America, an entire ocean will stand between us. Until now I could have come back to Berdichev, not safely, but still, I could have come back. Only land separated us.

Now there will be this great ocean between us. I can't swim across an ocean to get back to Berdichev. And you know something, Tovah? I don't want to.

I will work in America and find a way to do everything, everything, just as I told the Polish girl on the train from Motziv.

Maybe when I write and tell you how wonderful America is,

you will change your mind and come too, bringing the rest of our family with you out of Russia. Then we will all be together again. Aunt Anna, Uncle Avrum, Hannah, Bubbe Ruth, everyone. But especially you, Tovah.

Tovah and Rifka. Imagine it. Two clever girls in the United States of America.

Shalom, my dear cousin,
Rifka

We numbered many in the ship,
Some spread the sails, some pulled, together,
The mighty oars; 'twas placid weather.
The rudder in his steady grip,
Our helmsman silently was steering
The heavy galley through the sea,
While I, from doubts and sorrows free,
Sang to the crew . . .

—*Pushkin*

September 16, 1920
Somewhere on the Atlantic Ocean

Dear Tovah,
    The ship is excellent. I have a little room with a bed bolted to
the floor and a table that folds out. A small round window looks
out over the sea.
    But who wants to stay shut up in a cabin when there is so
much to do? Such a lounge there is, with a player piano and
polished wooden counters. The lounge reminds me of your salon
back in Berdichev, only much larger.
    There are dances at night and the passengers whirl about on
the parquet floor. During the day, a young sailor named Pieter
puts brushes on his feet and he dances all alone, polishing and
waxing. As he works, he sings and tells jokes to me.
    Out on the deck are chairs for days of reading. They are
bolted down like my bed so they won't shift in heavy seas. Of
course we've had nothing like heavy seas since we boarded.
Just clear skies and a gentle breeze.
    "Sometimes," Pieter says, "there are storms so fierce I think
the ship will break apart."
    Pieter is such a joker. I am never certain whether to believe
him or not.
    We trade songs and Pieter teaches me little dances when he is
not on watch. He is like another brother to me. Only he is better
somehow than a brother, though he teases every bit as much as

Saul does. But it doesn't annoy me when Pieter teases. I like it.

If I sit down in one of these chairs with our Pushkin, Pieter rushes over and tucks a blanket around my legs.

"Is there anything else I can do for you, Miss Rifka?" he asks.

He treats me like a little czarina. Me, Rifka Nebrot. Sometimes I pinch myself. Only in Hannah's games did I feel so special. How Hannah would love this. Tovah, you would too.

The ocean is so big; everywhere you look in every direction swells this dark, billowing water. It rises and falls as if it were breathing, and the ship skates over the surface.

I worried that perhaps I would feel seasick. I heard so many stories, and some others on the ship complain, but I do not feel the least bit ill. I feel healthier than I have ever felt in my entire life—even if I don't have any hair on my head.

Today I had the most interesting conversation with Pieter. He had a few minutes before he went on duty and we walked around the deck, talking. He told me he had nine brothers.

"No sisters?" I asked.

"No," he said. "Mama kept looking for a girl, but we kept coming out boys."

I told him about Isaac and Asher and Reuben and Nathan and Saul.

"And then there is me," I said.

"All those sons and then a daughter," Pieter said. "You are a treasure to your mama and papa. And to your brothers."

"I've never met my brothers Isaac and Asher and Reuben," I told Pieter. "They left for America before I was born. So I don't know if I am a treasure to them. But I assure you I am no treasure to my brother Saul. To Nathan maybe, but not to Saul."

Can you imagine, Tovah? Me, a treasure? I told Pieter, "Really, I don't believe anyone in my family thinks of *me* as a treasure."

Pieter said, "If this is true, then your family is blind."

I lowered my eyes for modesty's sake, but I couldn't help the smile that tugged at my lips, Tovah.

Pieter said, "You are such a brave girl, Rifka. And so clever to have managed on your own."

I had told him about our escape from Berdichev, and about the typhus, and how Mama and Papa had to leave me behind.

"I would not be so clever," Pieter said. "To learn so many languages. You speak Flemish better than I do and I have lived in Belgium all seventeen years of my life."

Again with the languages, Tovah. Why do people always make such a to-do?

"Pieter," I said. "You are full of nice words, but I am not certain I deserve them. You call me brave, but I will tell you what is brave. My aunt Anna is brave, and my little grandmother. They are brave to stay in Russia and live with the hatred for the Jews. They are clever, too, so much more clever. In Berdichev, you must be clever simply to stay alive.

"For me, since I've left Berdichev, life has been easy, except that I have been apart from Mama and Papa. I have met with such kindness. No, I am not so brave, Pieter. If I were brave, I would have stayed in Russia."

"Maybe," Pieter said, "maybe they are very brave, the ones you have left behind in your homeland. But are they clever?"

"My cousin Tovah is very clever," I told Pieter. "She has chosen to stay."

"I'm a simple boy," Pieter said. "I can't learn the speech of other countries the way you can. I only travel back and forth across this big ocean. I do not know much. But to me, Rifka, you seem very brave and very clever indeed."

Then Pieter bent over and kissed me! Right on my lips, Tovah. A warm kiss, with the soft blond hairs of his mustache tickling me.

Just for a moment I hoped the ship would never arrive in America and I could go on sailing with Pieter across this wide green ocean forever.

But when I looked up, Pieter's face was red. "I have work to do," he said, stammering. He hurried away, leaving me standing on the deck.

I don't understand. What did I do that Pieter should run away? How clever can I be, Tovah? The more I know, the more confused I get.

I returned to my cabin and opened our Pushkin. I tried to find a poem that said what I was feeling. Sometimes, when I read Pushkin's poems, I want to write poems of my own. I wonder if I dare to do such a thing. Saul always said I talked and talked without anything to say. But sometimes I do have something to say, and I feel as if I will explode if I don't write down what is in my head and in my heart.

Soon I will be in New York City, America. Soon I will be with Mama and Papa and all my giant brothers, Nathan and Saul, and Isaac and Asher and Reuben, brothers I don't even know.

In America, maybe, I will write poems.

> *Shalom, my cousin,*
> *Rifka*

... When suddenly,
A storm! And the wide sea was rearing . . .
The helmsman and the crew were lost.
No sailor by the storm was tossed
Ashore—but I, who had been singing.
I chant the songs I loved of yore,
And on the sunned and rocky shore
I dry my robes, all wet and clinging.

—Pushkin

September 21, 1920
Atlantic Ocean

Dear Tovah,

I have lost so much already, and now it seems I must lose more.

I nearly drowned at sea in a horrible storm. But I am alive. Everyone did not have my luck. But I am alive.

Our ship, which seemed so large and safe when first I boarded, barely survived the fury of this storm.

The tempest started during the night while we slept. I had dreams of pogroms, of cossacks on their horses, snapping whips at me, pointing rifles. I heard the crack of gunshot. In my dream the countryside was burning. I trembled in your cellar while the fire raged around me.

I woke from one terror into another. I had been thrown to the floor of my cabin, tossed from my bed by the rising seas.

Quickly I pulled on my clothes, tying my kerchief with trembling fingers. I opened my cabin door. Though it was still night, the sky was a sickly yellow, like an old bruise. I bashed against the ship's walls, flung back and forth by the tossing sea as I made my way toward the deck. The ship shivered in the hateful ocean. Twice the floor dropped beneath me suddenly, and I fell.

There was so much confusion on deck. No rain yet, but a wind that roared. The seas, which had seemed so gentle yesterday, rose like hungry beasts, mouths open, hovering and crashing over the sides of the ship.

Sailors ran like spiders, back and forth in the yellow light. They yelled to each other over the wind, shouting directions. Pieter, my Pieter, clung to a pillar as a wave broke over his shoulders.

All the horrors of Russia returned to me. The storm frightened me as much as any pogrom, when the peasants would come after the Jews to burn our homes, to break into our stores, to murder us.

My stomach twisted and I knew I would be sick, so I crawled, making my way with difficulty, toward the side of the ship. The ship rolled, my stomach rolled with it. I clung to the rail, trying to raise up off my knees so I would not soil myself with my own sickness. The ship plummeted from beneath me and I hit my head on the metal rail.

Someone came up behind me and wrapped a blanket around my shoulders.

"Pieter!" I cried.

I didn't realize the waves had drenched me.

"Come, Rifka!" Pieter yelled over the wind. "You must come away from the side."

I started shivering. I could taste blood in my mouth and smell it in my nose. It had a cold, metallic taste that made my stomach twist inside out. I tore away from Pieter's grip and ran back to the rail, emptying my stomach over the side.

Before I could finish, water, a wall of water, rose up over me. Pieter grabbed me around the waist and hurled me away from the side. The water came crashing down over our heads, slamming us onto the deck.

Pieter held on to me as the water sucked at my body, trying to pull me overboard. If he had not been there, Tovah, the ocean would have claimed me. He saved my life. Pieter held me until the wave lost its power and slipped away. Then he lifted me to my feet again before another monstrous wave could attack us.

"Come," he cried, guiding me toward a hatch. "Quickly. You must stay down in the hold while the storm lasts." Pieter shouted over the violent wind.

I descended into the ship's hold, looking up once at my friend. His hair lay plastered against his head and water streamed from his storm clothes.

"Pieter," I called, "are you putting me in steerage?"

Pieter laughed. "Brave and clever!" he called down to me. The wind screamed around him.

"Be careful, Pieter!" I cried.

"I will, Rifka," he answered.

I could hear the fear under the calm in his voice. It echoed in my ears as I stumbled down the ship's steep steps.

When I reached the bottom of the stairs, I found many of the other passengers already in the hold, huddled together. We were still equal. We were equally miserable, equally frightened for our lives.

Everyone got sick, even me. It stank worse than a flood of soured milk down there.

Women rocked back and forth weeping. Men held their stomachs and moaned. All the time I worried for Pieter and the others. I doubted, Tovah, that I would live to see my family again.

If I'd had the Pushkin, I could have read from it. I could have opened it to the pages that held my golden Star of David, woven from broom straws, and prayed for our lives on it. But the Pushkin remained above, in my cabin, and I could not go after it.

We shivered and sweated and retched for thirty-six hours, until the ship stopped its pitching. At last the hatch was opened and we climbed up out of our hole.

There was no more deck left to the ship. Everything once bolted down had been ripped away. The player piano had crashed against a wall and shattered into pieces.

Most of the deck chairs were gone too, torn right out of the floor. Twisted metal and bolts stuck up as signs of where the chairs had been.

The parquet tiles, what remained of them, were thick with filth from the sea.

A sailor lay on the deck, wrapped in gauze from head to toe, moaning. My heart jumped into my throat. What if it's Pieter? I thought. Oh, Tovah, if only I'd known.

I ran to the sailor's side, but it wasn't Pieter.

I asked if there was something I could do for him anyway. He didn't answer.

Other sailors were limping or bandaged. I looked for Pieter everywhere, but I couldn't find him.

Finally I stopped one of the officers.

"Have you seen the boy, Pieter?" I asked. "Please, I know you are busy, but could you tell me where I might find him?"

The officer looked down at me. He steadied my shoulders in his hands the way Papa had the night he told me of Uncle Zeb's death. "We lost one sailor overboard in the storm," he said.

"Pieter?" I whispered.

The officer nodded.

Tovah, I felt myself smothering. I couldn't see anything, hear anything.

Somehow I found my way back to my cabin, and for the first time since leaving Berdichev, I cried. All the tears that had collected in this year, in this enormous year, shoved their way out of my heart, and how I cried.

Pieter, who said I was so brave . . . what would he say to see me now?

I didn't care. I cried for Pieter, I cried for myself. I couldn't stop. I didn't want to stop.

I cried until I was empty of tears. Then I was still. As still as the sea after a storm.

I SIT in my cabin and wait. Our ship has sent out a distress call. It cannot move anymore on its own steam. The drum of the engines had been like a heartbeat. Now the heart has stopped. The engines are dead.

We must wait for another ship to answer our signal and tow us across the ocean to America. I pray there are no more storms between now and then. We could never survive another fight with the sea.

Tovah, suddenly I feel how defenseless we are—not just Jews, all of us. My mind fills with images of you and Aunt Anna and Bubbe Ruth and Mama and Papa. I see Bubbe Ruth at the rear of the long house, huddled beside her little stove, sipping tea from the samovar. I see Papa and Mama swallowed up by a strange country called America. I see you, Tovah, staring out the window at the empty road, the road that has carried me away from you. I realize how precious our lives are. And how brief. I want to come home.

The telegram the HIAS sent from Antwerp to Mama and Papa said I would be arriving in America today. Today I sit in the middle of the Atlantic Ocean on a ship that is dead.

What will happen when Papa and Mama come to get me and I'm not there? How will they know when to come back? Will I ever see them again?

I'm too tired, Tovah, too tired for all this trouble. At this moment I wish I had never left Berdichev.

Shalom, my Tovah,
Rifka

. . . And thoughts stir bravely in my head, and
rhymes
Run forth to meet them on light feet, and fingers
Reach for the pen . . .

—*Pushkin*

October 1, 1920
Entering New York Harbor

Dear Tovah,

Today we will arrive at Ellis Island. Today I will see Mama
and smell her yeasty smell. Today I will feel the tickle of Papa's
dark beard against my cheeks and see my brother Nathan's
dimpled smile and Saul's wild curly hair. Today I will meet my
brothers Asher and Isaac and Reuben.

Already I am wearing my best hat, the black velvet with the
shirring and the brim of light blue. I'm hoping that with the hat,
Mama will not mind my baldness. I've tucked Papa's tallis into
my rucksack, but Mama's gold locket hangs around my neck.

The captain said his company notified our families and they
are awaiting our arrival. I must pass a screening on the island
before I can go home with Mama and Papa. Papa wrote about
Ellis Island in his letters.

He wrote that at Ellis Island you are neither in nor out of
America. Ellis Island is a line separating my future from my past.
Until I cross that line, I am still homeless, still an immigrant.
Once I leave Ellis Island, though, I will truly be in America.

Papa said in his letter that they ask many questions at Ellis
Island. I must take my time and answer correctly. What's to
worry? I am good at answering questions. Even if they ask me a
thousand questions, I will have Mama and Papa near me, my
mama and papa.

Just one week ago, I did not think I would ever make it to
America. We drifted on the sea for days, helpless, waiting for the
ship to come and tow us. I assisted with the cleanup as best I
could, doing work Pieter would have done if he were there.

Then, once the tow ship arrived it took so long between the se-
curing of the ropes and the exchanges between the two ships, I

thought we would never begin moving. At last, when we did, the other ship pulled us so slowly. I could swim faster to America.

In Russia, all America meant to me was excitement, adventure. Now, coming to America means so much more. It is not simply a place you go when you run away. America is a place to begin anew.

In America, I think, life is as good as a clever girl can make it.

Very soon, Tovah, I will be in this America. I hope someday you will come, too.

Shalom, my cousin,
Rifka

P.S. As I was finishing this letter a cry went up from the deck. When I went out to see what it was, I found all the passengers gathered on one side of the ship, looking up. They were looking at Miss Liberty, Tovah, a great statue of a woman standing in the middle of the harbor. She was lifting a lamp to light the way for us.

. . . Give me your hand. I will return
At the beginning of October . . .
—*Pushkin*

October 2, 1920
Ellis Island

Dear Tovah,

I don't know how to tell about what has happened. I feel numb and I can't believe. I thought if I could tell you, maybe it would make some sense, maybe it would help.

They are holding me, detaining me on Ellis Island, at the hospital for contagious diseases. They won't let me go to Mama and Papa. They won't even let me see them. Tovah, I can't go to America!

After we landed, I sat on a bench in an enormous room with hundreds of others, waiting to hear my name called.

I waited a long time. I just wanted to see Mama and Papa. I kept looking around for them, for Mama's black hair, for Papa's beard, but they weren't there. There were others with thick beards, with dark hair, but they weren't my mama and papa. Certainly I would know my own mama and papa.

Finally a man called my name. I couldn't understand what he said to me. I felt nervous and he spoke English so fast, much faster than the lady from the HIAS. Someone found an interpreter for me. I answered their questions, I read from a book to prove I am not a simpleton, but they kept delaying my approval.

The doctor examined me. He took off my hat, my beautiful hat. I didn't like his taking off my hat any more than I liked the Russian guard touching my hair or the Polish doctor examining me at the border, but just as then, I had no choice.

The first doctor called over another doctor. They spoke fast. They looked at my scalp. They shook their heads. Then they called for a tall man with glasses. The nosepiece was dull with the mark of his thumbprint, so often did he shove the gold rims up on his thin nose.

"What is it?" I asked, pulling on the doctors' sleeves, but they didn't answer. The first doctor put a chalk mark on my shoulder and pointed me in the direction of a cage holding the detainees.

Detainees are immigrants who are not welcome in America. They remain on the island until the authorities decide what to do with them. People like criminals and simpletons are detainees. I didn't belong with them. I could not belong with them.

"Why are you holding me?" I cried in Yiddish. "Why have you put me with these people? I don't belong here. I belong in America. I have come to America."

A lady from the HIAS came over. She, too, was short, like the HIAS lady in Antwerp and the HIAS lady in Warsaw, but this one had a red bun on the top of her head.

"Shah," she said. "Don't make such a fuss. If you calm down, I will help you."

She spoke with the doctor. She spoke with the man who wore the gold-rimmed glasses. I saw her face grow less and less hopeful. When she walked back to me, I could tell it was not good news.

She explained to me in Yiddish what the doctors had said. "You must be kept in the hospital for contagious diseases. It's because of the ringworm you suffered from in Europe."

"They cured my ringworm!" I cried.

"Mr. Fargate, the tall man with the glasses, says he must be certain the ringworm is gone before you can enter the country," the lady from the HIAS said. "Perhaps it will only take a day or two."

"A day or two. I must go to Mama and Papa now! My papers say the ringworm is cured!" I cried. "Why don't they believe my papers? Why must I wait?"

"It's not just the ringworm that concerns them," said the lady from the HIAS. "It's your hair." She stroked my cheek with the back of her hand. She had a brown wart on her chin, with red hairs growing out of it. I pulled back from her.

"My hair?" I asked. I tugged at the black velvet hat, pulling it down until it nearly covered my ears.

"The doctors worry about your hair."

"Why should they worry over such a thing as my hair?" I asked.

"To them it is important," the HIAS lady said. "Even though your ringworm may be gone, if your hair does not grow back, Rifka, the American government will have to view you as a social responsibility."

"What does this mean? Social responsibility?" I asked.

"It means the American government is afraid they will have to support you for the rest of your life," the lady from the HIAS said. "Your lack of hair makes you an undesirable immigrant. They think without hair you will never find a husband to take care of you and so *they* will have to take care of you instead."

I couldn't believe what she was saying.

"Some Jewish women shave their heads on purpose," I said. "It is written into the Jewish law. To be bald is not a sin."

The HIAS lady sighed.

"You mean the country will not let me in simply because they are afraid when I grow up no one will want to marry me?"

"That is right."

"You don't need hair to be a good wife, do you?" I asked. "Jewish women wear wigs all the time. I could wear a wig and still be a good wife."

"You are a child," the lady from the HIAS said. "It is not that simple."

"It is that simple," I said.

She said, "I can't change the rules, Rifka. Either your hair grows or they will send you back."

There it was. What chance did I have of my hair growing now? It had not grown in almost a year.

Tovah, I think maybe you were wrong after all. You said a girl must not depend on her looks, that it is better to be clever. But in America looks are more important, and if it is my looks I must rely on, I am to be sent back. How can this be?

> *Shalom,*
> *Rifka*

. . . My path is bleak—before me stretch my
  morrows:
A tossing sea, foreboding toil and sorrows.
And yet I do not wish to die, be sure;
I want to live—think, suffer, and endure . . .
                              —*Pushkin*

October 7, 1920
Ellis Island

Dear Tovah,
　I have been here a week now. It is not so bad a place, really. I
am growing used to it. Crowds of people overfill the wards.
When they first brought me here, they gave me a choice. I could
sleep in a bed with another woman or by myself, in a crib. I
said, "I'll take the crib."
　My feet stuck out one end, but it was better than sleeping
with someone I didn't know. Someone who had a disease I didn't
want. Sometimes it is convenient I am small.
　There are so many of us here in the hospital. After two days, I
was transferred from one ward to another. In the new ward, I
got my own bed.
　Saul came to visit, but they sent him to the first ward and he
couldn't find me. No one could find me. So they sent Saul away.
　Saul would have been the first familiar face in almost a year. I
didn't care that it was just Saul. I would love to have seen Saul,
but they sent him away.
　When they did find me, they put me in still another ward.
Here a nurse has taken an interest in me.
　Her name is Nurse Bowen. Sometimes she takes me to her
room in a building on a different part of Ellis Island. We go in a
little boat to get there. I help her clean her apartment. Mostly,
though, I eat candy when I am there. She always has candy. It
is not as good as Belgian chocolate, but still it tastes very good.
I like going with her.
　I make better sense of English now. I listen to the nurses and
the doctors, following them on their rounds of the wards. I have

been able, even, to interpret a little for the Polish and Russian patients; only simple things, but the nurses and the doctors seem pleased to have me help them.

There is a little Polish baby here. She has no one. Her mama died of the typhus. Because I've already had the disease, I help take care of her. She is such a beautiful little thing, with dark eyes taking up half her face and a bald head, as bald as mine. She never fusses. I hold her and rock her and sing her Yiddish lullabies. I tell her stories and recite Pushkin to her. She reminds me a little of the baby on the train in Poland.

I have another responsibility. In the dining hall one night, a little boy sat across from me at the table. I couldn't tell what was wrong with him, why they were keeping him in the hospital, except that he was very thin and pale, with dark circles under his eyes. I looked in those eyes and remembered something, someone, but I was too hungry to give it much thought.

They served the food. It's not bad food, and there is so much of it. Hands went every which way, passing, dishing out, spooning in. But the little boy sat, watching it all go past him.

I helped myself to potatoes and meat and carrots and bread. The boy stared at my plate, but he took nothing for himself.

"What's the matter with you?" I asked in Yiddish. "Why don't you eat?"

He didn't answer.

"Eat," I said in English.

Still no answer.

"Take something to eat," I said in Russian.

Now he looked up at me, straight into my eyes.

"Russian you understand?" I said. "But not Yiddish?"

Then I knew. The boy was a peasant. A Russian peasant. Here, sitting before me, Tovah, was the reason we had fled our homeland. He was the reason for my being alone for so long, separated from my family. The reason I had had typhus. The reason I had lost my hair. The reason Uncle Zeb was dead and all your lives were in danger. I had him sitting in front of me in the dining hall of the hospital at Ellis Island.

I tried not to look at him. I did not want anything to do with him. But there he was, in front of me. A little Russian peasant.

He stared at his pale hands, folded in front of him at his place. Then he looked back up at me with those eyes.

I remembered then. He looked like a small version of the soldier at the train station, the one with the eyes of green ice. I didn't want anything to do with him. Nothing.

But no one should starve to death, Tovah. Certainly not a little boy, maybe seven years old.

"Is there something wrong with you that keeps you from eating?" I asked in Russian.

He shook his head.

"If you don't eat," I told him, "they will send you back."

He nodded.

"You want to go back?" I asked.

He nodded again, and this time tears filled his eyes.

"Well, just tell them you want to go back!" I cried.

If I go back, they will kill me. His father or his uncle, his cousin or his neighbor, they will make a pogrom, and they will kill me.

Crazy Russian peasant! He could stay here. He could stay here in America. There is nothing wrong with him. He could live in either place, Russia, America, and no harm would come to him. But no, he is starving himself so they will send him back.

People were eating all around us. The boy sat at his empty plate, tears rolling down his cheeks.

I hated him. I hated what he stood for.

I also hated seeing him cry. He was just a little boy.

"What's your name?" I asked.

"Ilya," he answered. His voice came out thin and high and frail.

"Ilya," I said. "If you don't eat anything, you will grow so weak that when they do send you back, you will die before you reach home. You must eat a little."

I stood up and looked for food to spoon onto his plate, but by now all the food bowls were empty.

What could I do? He was just a little boy, a hungry, frightened little boy. I lifted my plate and slid some of my own food onto his dish.

"Now eat," I said. "Or I will be hungry for nothing."

He put a little piece of carrot in his mouth and chewed. Then faster and faster he pushed the food in.

"Slow down," I said. "You'll get sick."

He finished everything on his plate, so I gave him a little more.

Maybe it is not very clever to feel what I felt about this Russian peasant, this enemy of my people.

But Tovah, he was just a little, hungry boy. Taking care of him made me feel better than I had felt in a very long time.

Ever since then, I have a shadow. He follows me everywhere,

holding on to my skirts. He sits by me when I rock the Polish baby, though I will not let him come too close. He follows me around the buildings, he sits under my elbow at mealtime, he is always under my feet.

The nurses call me the little mother. I don't mind so much.

What do you think about your cousin taking care of a little Russian peasant? You will probably think me the most foolish of all, to befriend such a child. I know Mama will not be happy, not the way she feels about everything Russian. I must figure out a way to explain to her when she comes to visit.

Oh, Tovah, how I hope she comes to visit soon.

> *Shalom,*
> *Rifka*

. . . I'm lean and shaven, but alive;
. . . And there is hope that I may thrive. . . .
—*Pushkin*

October 9, 1920
Ellis Island

Dear Tovah,

At last, I have seen someone from the family. I had started believing they weren't really here, that something terrible had happened to them and no one would tell me. I thought the Americans had stolen them away and imprisoned them and I would never see them again.

But Saul came. He skipped school and came to see me at the hospital.

"Mama and Papa and the others can't get away," he said in Yiddish. "They must all work. I thought I'd come."

Tovah, when I saw him—he's so big, so handsome—I almost cried.

But I wouldn't let Saul see me cry. He walked through the door and stood there, looking around the ward for me.

"Saul!" I called out. I ran to him and threw my arms around him.

He backed me away and looked down at me. "Rifka?"

"What's the matter?" I asked. "You don't recognize your own sister?"

He swallowed. I saw the knob in his big neck go up and down.

"You look different," Saul said.

I touched the kerchief covering my bald head.

"My hair," I said. "It's been gone a long time."

"No, it's not that," he said. "I don't remember your eyes being so big."

"I have the same eyes, Saul."

I took my brother by the hand and led him into the ward. I was glad to have a bed of my own when Saul came. It would embarrass me if he should learn I slept in a crib. He would never let me forget that.

"Here, I brought something for you."

Saul reached into his pocket and brought out a banana. His eyes twinkled with mischief.

I took the banana and peeled it and started to bite into it. Then I remembered how he had shared with me in Motziv, and I offered him the first bite. He shook his head. The sparkle had gone from his eyes. He looked disappointed.

"What's the matter, Saul?" I asked.

"How did you know to do that?" Saul asked.

"How did you know to peel the banana? In Russia, we didn't see bananas."

I laughed. "Is that what's worrying you? There are lots of bananas in Antwerp," I told him. "And chocolates, and ice cream, too."

"Humph," Saul said. "I guess you're not such a greenhorn."

"What's a greenhorn?" I asked.

"It's when you come off the boat and you don't know what a banana is," Saul said.

"Well, I guess I'm not a greenhorn, then."

Saul was dressed like a dandy. He wore knickers and a stiff shirt. A cap sat cocked on his head. He was showing off in front of me. He wanted me to say something nice about his clothes. But he had hoped to make a fool of me with that banana. I didn't want him to know how handsome I thought he looked. My American brother.

When Doctor Askin came by on his rounds, I spoke English, introducing the doctor to Saul.

Doctor Askin said, "It's a pleasure to meet you, young man."

Saul, my giant brother Saul, looked down at his big feet and said nothing. His ears turned red.

"Saul," I said, kicking his shoe with my boot.

Still Saul said nothing.

"He is happy to meet you too, Doctor Askin," I said. "Are you not, Saul?"

Saul nodded. Doctor Askin said good-bye and walked away.

"Doctor Askin is my friend," I told Saul, still speaking in English. "Why did you not talk to him? He is a good man. He brings the comics here. We look at the pictures. I can read a little."

"You *read* English too?" Saul asked.

"A little," I said. "I am learning each day. Nurse Bowen helps. Doctor Askin helps too, before he and Mr. Fargate talk about patients."

"Your English," Saul said, "is very good. Where did you learn to speak this way, Rifka? You learned this in Antwerp too?"

"Yes," I told him. "I learned much in Antwerp."

Saul looked at me with his head tilted to one side. "My sister

Rifka speaks like an American in one week?"

"Nine days," I said. "I've been here nine days."

"Smarty," he said. He lifted his hand to tousle my hair, something he used to do when I had blond curls, back in Russia.

Saul pulled his hand back before he touched the kerchief hiding my bald head.

"What should I tell Mama about your hair?" he asked.

"Tell her the truth," I said. "It's not growing. Why should it grow now? It hasn't grown in a year."

Saul looked down at his feet. "So they will send you back?"

I didn't know what to say.

Saul looked so big and healthy and uncomfortable in the busy hospital ward. I smiled at him. "If I have to go back, Saul, I'm sure I can stay with Bubbe Ruth. Or Uncle Avrum and Tovah and Hannah. It won't be so bad for me."

Saul and I both knew the truth. We'd left Berdichev to save his life. Because of this, I might very well lose mine.

Just then, Ilya appeared, wiggling his way under my arm. I introduced him to Saul in English. "This is my little friend," I said. "He also comes from Russia."

Saul noticed the book of Pushkin that Ilya pulled out from under my pillow. Ilya likes when I read Pushkin to him, especially in the afternoon when things quiet down for a little while around the ward.

"What have you got there?" Saul asked Ilya in Yiddish.

Ilya did not answer. He looked frightened of Saul.

Saul took the book from him.

Ilya's eyes flashed with anger.

"Ilya," I said in Russian. "This is my brother."

Ilya looked from me to Saul, but he is a stubborn little boy. He tried to get the book back from Saul. Between the two pulling on it, Tovah, the Pushkin dropped and fell open. My Star of David, the one I had woven from broom straws in Antwerp, bounced off the floor and broke apart.

Ilya knew how precious the little straw star had been to me. Always, he had handled it with such care. He looked into my face, blinked his green eyes, and then ran out of the ward.

"He's a nasty little peasant," Saul said. "I don't believe you, Rifka. What are you doing with a peasant? And this book. Throw it away. It's a Russian book! And what is all this scribbling inside?"

"Leave it alone, Saul," I said, grabbing the book and holding it tight to my chest. I was angry at him. He had broken my star.

But I was angry at him for more than that. Inside, it felt like much more than that.

"You can't tell me what I should throw away," I said. It hurt deep in my heart, Tovah, but at this moment I loved Ilya more than I loved my own brother. "This book, it's mine—"

Saul grabbed for the book again, but I stood my ground, squeezing the hard cover against my ribs.

"You're different, Rifka," Saul said.

"I am the same, Saul," I cried. "Still, my life has gone on while we've been apart. I am older in many ways since you left me in Warsaw."

"You're still my little sister, though," Saul said.

Saul's dark eyes burned with anger, but something else burned there too. I remembered Pieter and what he'd said about my being a treasure to my brothers.

I put my hand on Saul's sleeve. "Yes. I am still your little sister. Let's not fight, Saul. I have been so lonely. You haven't even told me anything about Mama or Papa or Nathan and the others. Please stay and talk with me."

Saul looked as if he was still angry, but he sat back down. My cot groaned under his weight.

"Papa and Mama work all day at the clothing factory," Saul said. "When they come home at night, they bring bags of trousers to hem. They work together until late. I help, but I can't stay awake so long to finish."

Mama and Papa—working so hard? They needed my help. Couldn't the Americans see how much my family needed me?

"What about Nathan?" I asked.

"Nathan has a job in a bakery. He leaves before light and comes home after dark, his clothes always covered with flour."

"And you?"

"I go to school," Saul said. "Papa says I must get an education. I'd rather be working, but Papa says no. If you were with us, Rifka, maybe he would let me work. Maybe it would be enough for you to go to school. But . . ."

Saul didn't finish. None of us had any say about whether I could come to join my family and go to an American school. I wanted nothing more than that.

But only Mr. Fargate could decide.

Saul said, "Isaac married a girl named Sadie. Sadie Chenowitz, of the Berdichev Chenowitzes."

What a small world, Tovah. My oldest brother, Isaac, comes all the way from Russia and who does he pick to marry but a landsman, a girl from our own village, a Chenowitz girl.

"She's very pretty," Saul said.

He said Isaac and Sadie had a baby boy named Aaron.

"That makes me an aunt," I said, clapping my hands. "Can you believe it? Me, Aunt Rifka." I wanted to hold my brother Isaac's baby, right that instant.

"Did Mama ever get new candlesticks?" I asked.

Saul said they could not afford to buy candlesticks. He said everything they earned they sent to me in Belgium. My dear family, how much they had given up for me.

"What do you do on the Sabbath?" I asked.

"We work on the Sabbath," Saul said.

I couldn't believe my ears. Mama, Papa, working on the Sabbath?

I opened my rucksack and took out my pouch of money.

"Where did you get all this, Rifka?" Saul asked.

"I saved it," I said. "From the money Papa sent."

"Papa sent that money for you to eat, Rifka. What did you eat?"

"I ate, Saul," I said. I wasn't about to tell him *what* I ate.

"I want you to take this money, Saul," I said. "I want you to take it and buy candlesticks for Mama. If there is any money left, tell Mama and Papa to use it so they do not have to work on the Sabbath. Do you hear me, Saul?"

Saul promised about the candlesticks. He apologized for breaking my star. Then he was gone. I had forgotten how lonely I'd been until he was gone.

Tovah, I have never seen my brother Isaac. He fled Russia before I was born. Now I wonder if I ever will see him, or his baby. Would they send me back, do you think, without ever holding my brother's baby?

> *Shalom,*
> *Rifka*

... They say ill things of the last days of Autumn:
But I, friend reader, not a one will hear;
Her quiet beauty touches me as surely
As does a wistful child, to no one dear. ...

—*Pushkin*

October 11, 1920
Ellis Island

Dear Tovah,

Mama came today.

My wonderful, beautiful Mama. She hugged me and kissed me and I smelled onion on her and chicken and celery and yeast. I was so happy I thought my heart had broken open like an egg.

"Mama," I kept repeating, afraid I would blink and she would no longer be sitting beside me on my cot.

Mama brought out a tiny honey cake. "For your thirteenth birthday," she said in Yiddish.

She watched me eat it, the whole thing, as we sat close together on the edge of my bed. I licked each finger. It tasted as good as I remembered, Mama's honey cake.

"Tell me about Antwerp," Mama said.

I told her about Sister Katrina and the lady from the HIAS and Gizelle in the park. I told her about the awful storm at sea, and how our ship needed towing to Ellis Island.

"What about your hair?" Mama asked. "Is it really so bad?"

Mama led me over to the window and took off my kerchief. She examined my scalp. I felt envy for the long black hair coiled around her ears.

She sighed and rested her hand on my naked head.

"Please," I said, removing her hand.

I carefully tied the kerchief back on.

"I wish your bubbe were here," Mama said. "Your bubbe would know what to do."

"I wish she were here too, Mama," I answered back.

I wish you were here too, Tovah, but now I don't know if that is such a good idea. You have to be perfect to come to America. I have this bald head and you, you have a crooked back. We are not perfect. We are not welcome.

"These Americans," I told Mama. "They don't make any sense. They say they are holding me because I am too contagious to come into their country, but they allow you to visit me. If I'm contagious, won't I make you sick? And if I make you sick, won't you make everyone else in America sick? What's the difference if I go to New York or you come here? Either way, if I really am contagious, somebody is going to get sick. I'm wondering how clever these Americans really are."

"Hush, Rifka," Mama said. "Somebody could hear you."

I looked around. Even if they did speak Yiddish, no one around us was listening.

"Why is such a great country like America afraid of a little Jewish girl just because she doesn't have any hair on her head?" I said. "The truth, Mama, is that they're afraid I will never find a husband. As if I need hair to get married."

"Maybe we could rub something in to make your hair grow," Mama said. "I wish Papa could come. He would have some ideas."

"It's no good, Mama," I said. "Not even Papa can get my hair to grow. I am bald."

"But Rifka," Mama said.

Then she didn't say anything more. What could she say? I am bald.

"Don't worry, Mama."

Mama never was very good with doctoring. Always Papa nursed us through sickness.

"Are you eating right?" Mama wanted to know.

"The food is very good here."

I didn't tell her about all the chocolate and ice cream I ate in Belgium.

Doctor Askin came and said hello to Mama. Then he joined Mr. Fargate for the case reviews.

I was telling Mama about the market in Antwerp when my little Polish baby began crying.

"Excuse me, please, Mama," I said. I left Mama sitting on my bed. I didn't want to leave her. I didn't want to lose one precious second with her, but the baby needed me.

As soon as I settled the baby down, a fevered woman asked for water. Then there were other chores that needed doing, things I helped the nurses with every day. I kept looking over to Mama, afraid she would disappear.

She didn't disappear. She sat and watched.

"Just like Papa," she said when I finally got back to her. "And the way you speak English, Rifka. You've always been good with languages. You were talking before you could walk. But I never imagined you could learn English so quickly. I have been here a year. I hardly speak a word."

"I could help you," I told Mama, "if they allow me to stay."

"Who is the baby?" Mama asked.

I took Mama's hand and led her over to the crib.

I said. "She is Polish. Her mother died of the typhus. The baby has the typhus too. See." I showed Mama the rash. "I help take care of her."

Ilya, I noticed, kept his distance the whole of Mama's visit. Usually he clung to me like a drop of sap. He was even jealous when I held the baby.

Maybe Ilya understood something about Mama.

Tovah, you would be accepting of my friendship with Ilya. Uncle Avrum has Russian friends, non-Jewish friends. But Mama and Papa, they wouldn't like it at all.

Mama can be more accepting of the Polish baby. A baby that speaks no language. It could be a Jewish baby, after all. There are many Polish Jews. But Ilya is no Jew. He is a Russian peasant, and Mama and Papa have grown to hate everything Russian.

I have been thinking, Tovah. To turn my back on the part of me that is Russian is impossible. I am Jewish, yes, but I am Russian too. I am both Jewish and Russian. And I am also more. I am so much more.

When I read the poetry of Pushkin to Ilya and watch his face, I can see the words rocking him the way they do me. We both ache for something we have lost.

Yet he aches in a way that I cannot imagine. At least I still have family. In Russia and in America, I have family who love me and want me. Even Saul wants me, in his own way.

For Ilya, there is no family. In America there is an uncle, an uncle who works three jobs and wants Ilya not because he loves him, but because of the money Ilya can earn. Not once since I've been here has the uncle come to visit Ilya. Not once. Is this the way family behaves?

Poor Ilya, he cannot get back his old life in Russia. Ilya's mother became widowed when he was two. When she remarried, her new husband did not want Ilya. That is why she sent him to America. Ilya can't go back. At least not to his own people. Maybe you and Hannah would take him in. Could you raise a little Russian boy?

No, of course not. You would tell me the wisest thing to do

would be to help Ilya prepare for America. He has no choice but to come into America.

He's a smart boy. He knows the poetry of Pushkin by heart. I have read to him so often that now he reads passages himself.

I tell him, "Ilya, you should be learning to read English, not Russian. You are going to be an American."

He looks at me with those stormy eyes. Sometimes he looks so lost.

We are trapped between two worlds, Ilya and I. Ilya wants to go back to Russia, to the only place he has ever known. I want to enter America. Yet neither of us can leave this island.

Ilya is eating and the circles lessen under his eyes, but still he is thin and frail. I think the doctors and Mr. Fargate are more concerned with his mind, though, than with his health.

They think Ilya is a simpleton—because he won't take food for himself. I am still putting food on his plate. And he never talks to anyone else. He talks only to me, when no one is listening. But he is very smart, Tovah. Any seven-year-old who can read Pushkin is one clever boy. I must help him see that his life is here, in America, not back in Russia. How do I do that?

Tovah, you would know.

My dear cousin, I miss you like soup misses salt.

> *Shalom,*
> *Rifka*

... Oh, mournful season that delights the eyes,
Your farewell beauty captivates my spirit.
I love the pomp of Nature's fading dyes,
The forests, garmented in gold and purple,
The rush of noisy wind, and the pale skies
Half-hidden by the clouds in darkling billows,
And the rare sun-ray and the early frost,
And threats of grizzled Winter, heard and lost. ...

—Pushkin

October 14, 1920
Ellis Island

Dear Tovah,

Ilya got me into such trouble today. We were walking through a part of the hospital we didn't know very well. We heard the *d-d-d-d* of a machine. Ilya loves machines. He dragged me over to the place where some men were working on a balcony overlooking the harbor.

I stepped closer to the workmen. One of them used English words I hadn't heard before. I don't think they were words Mama would want me to learn, but still I was curious.

All of a sudden I realized Ilya was missing. He is never more than a step or two away from me. Now for the first time in weeks he had disappeared from my sight.

I rushed toward the balcony, calling for him. A little boy could easily fall over the edge into the water. I ran from the balcony to the hallway, then back again, fretting in Russian. The workmen stopped their hammers to stare at me.

It took a moment for the sound of their machines to stop inside my head, but then, in the silence, I heard Ilya's high voice, crying out.

I turned toward the sound. There stood a row of metal toilet stalls. It was from the stalls that Ilya's voice came. Inside one I found him. He had his back to me, and clouds of white paper flew over his head as if some great white bird were descending on him.

But it was no bird. Ilya was unrolling toilet paper, an endless ribbon of it. As he unwound it, he laughed wildly. He cried, "Paper! Paper!"

I scolded him in Russian. I yelled for him to stop.

"Look what you are doing, Ilya. You are going to get us killed. Look how you are wasting the paper."

I grabbed his arm, holding it away, while frantically I started rolling the paper back. I was trying to wind it up so no one would punish us and I was yelling at him in Russian.

One of the workers started toward us. He pushed his big arm into the stall past me and Ilya. The worker ripped out the roll of toilet paper, throwing it over the rail and into the harbor. The white tail of Ilya's unravelings sailed over our heads and disappeared beyond the balcony.

The worker looked as though he would next pitch us into the harbor.

Well, I grabbed Ilya and I ran with him so fast he cracked his shoulder against a wall. I didn't stop to comfort him.

"We're going to get killed!" I cried, pulling him, checking over my shoulder every few seconds to see if the man was chasing us.

"Don't you ever do that again," I told Ilya, trying to catch my breath. We collapsed on my cot.

Nurse Bowen came over. Ilya held his shoulder and wept.

"What happened?" the nurse asked, examining Ilya's shoulder.

"Promise you won't tell Mr. Fargate?" I asked. "Promise you won't let him send us back to Russia."

"Tell me, Rifka," the nurse said.

"Ilya unrolled toilet paper," I said, believing Ilya had committed one of the worse offenses he could ever commit here.

"Toilet paper?" the nurse asked. "What are you talking about, Rifka?"

I told her about the stalls and the workmen.

Nurse Bowen started laughing.

"This is not funny," I told her. "In Russia, to waste paper is a terrible crime."

"Well, in America it's not, Rifka," Nurse Bowen said. "There is plenty of paper. Toilet paper, newspaper, every kind of paper. Don't worry. We're not going to send you back to Russia over a roll of toilet paper."

She told me to tell Ilya that his shoulder would be fine. Already he had stopped crying.

Nurse Bowen went away, still laughing.

I felt a little insulted that she should laugh at me. But if paper was not so precious here, maybe it was a little funny. Maybe. And maybe I could get some of that plentiful paper Nurse Bowen talked about to write on.

Ilya slid the Pushkin out from under my pillow. He handed it to me to read to him.

I said, "No, no Pushkin. I'm going to write a poem of my own."

Remember, Tovah, when I said I might try? Well, I've been writing a little at the back of our book. There is hardly any room left between my letters to you and my poetry, but still I keep writing. Sometimes even in English. It is not very good poetry. Mostly, it doesn't rhyme, but I write anyway. I write poems about Russia and Bubbe Ruth and you and Hannah and coming to America and Ellis Island.

I asked Nurse Bowen for some of that paper she was talking about. She gave me a handful.

A handful of paper, Tovah. The paper alone is enough to draw the words from inside me. I took the paper and our Pushkin outside. Ilya, of course, followed behind me like a shadow.

It is pretty here on the island. Across the harbor, tall buildings stand like giant guards, blocking my way to Mama and Papa. I fear those guards will never let me pass. Yet even in my fear I cannot deny the beauty of this place.

The leaves change color just as they do in Berdichev. Geese fly overhead, honking, forming and reforming in the blue sky above Miss Liberty. The sun feels warm on my shoulders and the smell of autumn tickles my nose.

My writing maybe is not as beautiful as Pushkin's, but it comforts me. Ilya likes it too. He makes me read my poems over and over to him. It is nice to have an audience.

You didn't know I would turn out to be a poet, did you, Tovah? Is that being clever?

Shalom, my cousin,
Rifka

. . . This heart its leave of you has taken;
Accept, my distant dear, love's close,
As does the wife death leaves forsaken,
As does the exile's comrade, shaken
And mute, who clasps him once, and goes.

—*Pushkin*

October 21, 1920
Ellis Island

Dear Tovah,

The baby with the typhus, the baby I have taken care of since I got here three weeks ago, I found her in her crib this morning, Tovah. I found her dead.

She died during the night, alone. I remember how her dark eyes would look straight inside me. She would hold on to my finger with her tiny fist and squeeze as if she could squeeze my strength into her. I gave her my strength, gladly, all that I could give her. It wasn't enough. I loved that little baby, Tovah.

Now Mr. Fargate comes in. He says he has let my family know that tomorrow he will decide about my case. So tomorrow I learn what will become of me. Mr. Fargate has called Ilya's uncle too.

I'm so frightened, Tovah. More than an ocean separates me from Berdichev now. Inside me, something has changed. I can't go back.

Worst of all, my head has begun itching again. It started a day or so ago. I am afraid to lift off my scarf and look at it. I couldn't bear to see sores covering my scalp again.

So the ringworm isn't gone after all. If they check, they will send me back for sure.

I should have just remained in Russia as you did, Tovah. That would have been the wisest thing of all. The thought of going back across the ocean, across Europe, through Poland, back to Berdichev . . . it is too much for me to bear.

To leave America without ever having a chance at it, to leave Mama and Papa and all my big brothers when I know how much they need me, I can't let myself think of it.

Even if I could travel all those miles, even if I managed to find my way back, even if the Russians did not kill me, I couldn't live in Berdichev again. I have lived too much in this big world to go back to Berdichev.

Shalom, Tovah,
Rifka

. . . The heavy-hanging chains will fall,
The walls will crumble at a word;
And Freedom greet you in the light,
And brothers give you back the sword.

—Pushkin

October 22, 1920
Ellis Island

Dear Tovah,

This is the last letter I will ever write you from Ellis Island. It is almost impossible to believe what has happened today. I don't know where to start.

I woke up feeling like a lump of wool had caught in my throat. I let Ilya sleep in bed beside me last night. I knew it was probably our last night together, whatever happened.

We whispered for a long time in the dark. I told him not to be afraid of America. That he would make friends here. That his uncle would love him and take care of him.

I told him that in Russia, he would always be a peasant. That would never change. He would die young just as his father had and maybe leave a little boy just as his father had left him. I told him in America, he could grow up to be anything he wanted. He could have a wife and children and live to be an old man and see his grandchildren born.

He said he would stay, if he could marry me.

That made me smile. I'm glad it was dark so he couldn't see. I didn't want him to think I was making fun.

I have learned so much about America in these three weeks. It is hard to believe I got so upset over Ilya and the toilet paper just a few days ago. I laugh about it now. I understand so much more.

Yet as I woke this morning, with Ilya curled up beside me, I wondered what good would come from my understanding. What chance did I have of staying? Not only did I have no hair, but the ringworm had returned. Every second I had to remind myself not to scratch at the ringworm.

Ilya had America within his grasp, but me, I held nothing. I held only Russia.

Mr. Fargate, the man who makes these decisions, came into the little office beside the ward. He called Ilya in first.

Ilya gripped my hand and pulled me into the office with him. Mr. Fargate and Doctor Askin discussed Ilya, examined him. Mr. Fargate noticed that Ilya had gained weight.

Ilya's uncle sat in a chair nearby. He was such a little man, with thin blond hair and stormy eyes, just like Ilya's.

My family, my whole beautiful family, Papa and Mama and Saul, and Nathan and Asher and Reuben, and Isaac and Sadie and the little baby, Aaron, they were all there too. How I longed to be with them. I looked at each of them, memorizing their faces. My brothers Reuben and Asher and Isaac, I would have known them anywhere. Isaac and Asher look just like Papa, and Reuben, he looks like me. When they first arrived, I hugged and kissed them all.

I whispered to Saul, "Did you get the candlesticks?"

He said, "Yes, Rifka. But I have not given them to Mama yet."

"What are you waiting for?" I asked.

Saul shrugged.

Now I could only look at my family from a distance. Ilya needed me.

Ilya's uncle cowered under the giant shadow of my family. When Nurse Bowen passed him, his hair lifted off his high forehead in the little breeze that she made. He held his hat in his hand, his fingers inching around the brim over and over again, his shoulders hunched. It looked to me like he needed Ilya as much as Ilya needed him.

Mr. Fargate said, "This boy shows minimal intelligence. He doesn't feed himself, he doesn't speak. Has there been any change since his last review, Doctor Askin?"

The doctor said many things, but the more he talked the more clear it became he didn't know Ilya at all.

He believed Ilya *was* a simpleton.

Ilya could read Pushkin. He was smart enough to figure out if he starved himself, he'd get shipped back home. That's not a simpleton. They couldn't send him back for being a simpleton.

Mr. Fargate pushed his glasses up on his nose and leaned over his desk to peer at Ilya.

"Can you speak?" he asked in English.

Ilya stared straight into Mr. Fargate's eyes, but he said nothing.

"He doesn't understand English," Nurse Bowen said.

Mr. Fargate nodded. "Find someone who can translate."

"I can," I offered.

Mr. Fargate looked over his glasses at me. "Ask the boy if he can talk," said Mr. Fargate.

"Talk," I told Ilya in Russian.

Ilya glared at me.

"Ilya, talk!"

Ilya slowly shook his head.

"Go get my Pushkin," I told Ilya.

He looked up at me and brushed his blond hair out of his eyes. His uncle looked up at me too, startled.

"Go on, get the book," I repeated.

Ilya was being as stubborn as ever. He stood in his place and refused to move.

"Ilya," I commanded. "Go over there and get the book of Pushkin. Now!"

I pointed toward my cot.

Ilya stared at me with those stormy green eyes. Then he lowered his chin, brushed past his uncle, and got the book.

"Ilya is a smart boy," I told Mr. Fargate in English.

I looked down at Ilya. "Read to them," I ordered in Russian. "Show them that you are smart enough to live in America. I know how clever you are, Ilya. But Mr. Fargate needs to know. Your uncle needs to know too."

I looked back to where the uncle sat with his hat in his lap. The man's eyes never left Ilya. He drank in the sight of his nephew the way a thirsty man pulls at a dipper of water.

Still, Ilya remained silent.

Mr. Fargate lifted the stamp, the deportation stamp.

"Please," I begged Ilya's uncle in Russian. "You are losing him. He must prove to them that he is not a simpleton or they will send him away."

I tried to get the uncle to understand.

"He is afraid of you. He thinks you don't want him."

"He is my sister's son," Ilya's uncle said in Russian. "Of course I want him. He is my flesh and blood. I sent for him to give him a better life here in America. I work day and night so he can have a good life."

"Do you hear, Ilya?" I said. "Do you hear?"

Ilya turned his eyes for the first time on his uncle.

"Doctor Askin," I said in English. "Ilya is not a simpleton. I know he won't talk to you. But he *can* talk. He can read, too. He is only seven years, but he can read."

I gave Ilya the book. "Now read," I commanded in Russian.

Ilya's uncle got up out of his seat and came over. He put his hat down on the edge of Mr. Fargate's desk and knelt before his nephew. "Please, Ilya," he said. "Do what your friend says."

Ilya brushed the blond hair up onto his forehead. Then he began to read.

"Storm-clouds dim the sky; the tempest
Weaves the snow in patterns wild . . ."

Ilya's voice shook, but he was reading.

"Like a beast the gale is howling,
And now wailing like a child . . ."

Tears filled the eyes of Ilya's uncle.

"Is he reading?" Mr. Fargate asked. "Is that Russian?"

Ilya's uncle nodded. "Pushkin."

"Let me see the book a moment," Mr. Fargate said. He reached for the Pushkin. Ilya pulled it back, clasping the book to his chest.

"Show Mr. Fargate the book," I said in Russian. "Go on, Ilya."

Ilya's hands trembled as he handed the book to Mr. Fargate. Mr. Fargate opened our Pushkin to another page. "Read this."

". . . I like the grapes whose clusters ripen
Upon the hillside in the sun . . ."

Ilya's finger dragged across the page as he read the words.

I smiled. Doctor Askin smiled. Nurse Bowen smiled too.

"He understands this?" Mr. Fargate said. "At the age of seven?"

"Yes, sir," I said. "He understands."

Mr. Fargate lifted the stamp that permitted Ilya to enter the country and thumped it down on Ilya's papers. Ilya was going to stay in America.

"Did I do it right, Rifka?" he asked in Russian.

"Yes, Ilya," I said. "You did it just right."

Ilya's uncle still knelt on the floor beside us. His arms opened up to take Ilya in. Oh, Tovah. You should have seen the way Ilya and his uncle embraced. In all the times he clung to me, Ilya never held me in such a way. Never.

Ilya had attracted a lot of attention on the ward. No one but myself had ever heard his voice. Now there he was, reading Pushkin. Other nurses and doctors came over. They stood around in wonder at Ilya, now jabbering in Russian as he led his uncle back to his cot.

I could not listen to what they were saying. The time had come for my review. My family waited tensely, some sitting, some standing, waiting for a decision about me. If only I could melt into their tight strong circle, but now, as I had so often over the last year, I stood alone.

Mr. Fargate was talking with Doctor Askin about me. He wanted to know about the ringworm.

"She arrived fully cured," Doctor Askin said. "They made sure she was clean in Belgium before they sent her."

Please, I prayed. Don't let them check for the ringworm now.

They hadn't checked in over a week. I'd shown no sign of being infectious for so long, they believed the ringworm was gone.

I bit the insides of my cheeks to keep from scratching my itchy scalp. In my head, I repeated Sister Mary Katherine's prayer; I repeated a few Hebrew prayers too.

Mr. Fargate turned to Doctor Askin. "What about her hair? Is there any sign of growth?"

I slipped my hand up to my kerchief and gave a quick scratch. I tried not to, but I couldn't keep my hand away from it. It itched so badly. It had been itching all morning.

"Here, Rifka," Doctor Askin said kindly, starting to unknot my kerchief. "Let me look once more to see if there is any sign of hair."

I pulled away.

Oh, Tovah, if ever I needed to be clever, it was now.

"You know," I said. "What does it matter if my hair grows? A girl can not depend on her looks. It is better to be clever. I learned to speak English in three weeks, you know."

"Yes, I know," Mr. Fargate replied.

"I help here too," I said. "I am a good worker."

Mr. Fargate's eyeglasses slid down to the tip of his nose and he stared over them at me. "Not very modest, is she?"

They all laughed.

"It is true!" I cried. "I *am* a good worker!"

"You are, Rifka," Doctor Askin agreed. He turned to Mr. Fargate. "With the right opportunity, the girl could study medicine. She has skill and talent."

"In your opinion, then," Mr. Fargate said, "she would not end up a ward of the state?"

"Who can tell?" said the doctor. "But the opposite is more likely. I have seen her care for the patients. Compassion is a part of medicine you can't teach, Mr. Fargate. Compassion is a quality I have often seen in Rifka. Look what she did for the boy."

"I still worry about her hair," Mr. Fargate said.

I looked Mr. Fargate right in the eye. "I do not need hair to get a good life," I said.

"Maybe right now you don't," Mr. Fargate answered. "But what about when you wish to marry?"

"If I wish to marry, Mr. Fargate," I said—can you believe I spoke like this to an American official, Tovah?—"if I wish to marry, I will do so with hair or without hair."

I heard Mama gasp. This much English she understood.

Mr. Fargate leaned forward to study me. He stared at me through the glasses balanced at the bottom of his nose.

"You have plenty to say, young lady," Mr. Fargate said.

"Yes," I agreed, "I do."

"Oy, Rifka," Mama whispered.

I turned toward Mama. What I saw, though, was my brother Saul kneeling beside Ilya. Ilya and Saul were looking at the book of Pushkin together. Then Saul stood and took Ilya's hand and they approached Mr. Fargate.

"Yes?" Mr. Fargate asked.

Ilya looked up at me. "Read to them," he commanded in Russian.

"Ilya, that will not work for me," I told him in his own language. "They already know I can read. My case is not the same as yours."

"Read to them your poetry," Saul said. "The words you have written in the back of this book."

I looked hard at Ilya. "You had no right to show that to anyone," I said. "Those are my words."

"They are good words, Rifka," Saul said.

"They are nothing," I answered. "Simple little poems. They don't even rhyme. What good would it do to read such things aloud? Leave it be."

Ilya would not leave it.

He took the Pushkin and elbowed in front of me to stand under the stern eye of Mr. Fargate.

"This," he said, speaking English with a very thick accent. "This Rifka write."

I'd never heard him speak anything but Russian before.

He took a deep breath and let it out. He swallowed once, hard. Then he began reciting my latest poem in English. How I had struggled with the words. Ilya had made me repeat them to him each time I stopped or changed something. Now he remembered it perfectly. He didn't look at the book. He just held it in front of him and said the poem from memory.

"I leave to you the low and leaning room,
where once we drank the honey-sweetened tea,
and bowed our heads in prayer and waited there,
for cossacks with their boots and bayonets."

They were all listening, even Ilya's uncle.

"I leave behind my cousins, young and dear;
They'll never know the freedom I have known,
Or learn as I have learned, that kindness dwells,
In hearts that have no fear."

"You wrote these words?" Mr. Fargate asked.

I nodded, embarrassed.

"Rifka Nebrot," Mr. Fargate said. "This is a very nice poem."

"You think?" I asked. "That is just one poem." I took the book from Ilya and started turning pages. "I have more, Mr. Fargate, many more. I can read to you. Do you have time? Here is one you will like, I think . . ."

Mr. Fargate looked at his watch. Then he looked at Doctor Askin. "No wonder the boy never talked. She talks enough for both of them."

Now, I thought, it would be clever to keep quiet.

"Well, Miss Nebrot," Mr. Fargate said. "After giving the matter some consideration, I think you are correct. Whether you wish to marry or not is no business of mine." He turned to Doctor Askin. "Heaven help the man she does marry."

Turning back to me, he said, "I have no doubt that if you wish to marry, you will manage to do so, whether you have hair or not."

Then he looked over to Mama and Papa. "Mr. and Mrs. Nebrot. These are your daughter's papers. With this stamp I give permission for her to enter the United States of America."

My heart thundered in my chest.

Mr. Fargate stamped my entrance papers and handed them to me. "Here, Rifka Nebrot," he said. "Welcome to America."

The nurses and doctors swept over me. Ilya, too. Best of all my family, my beloved family, Saul, Nathan, Reuben, Asher, Isaac, Mama, Papa, Sadie, and little Aaron. There was such a commotion with all the kissing and the hugging I could hardly breathe.

Then I felt something that made me stiffen with fear. In all the kissing and hugging, someone had loosened the kerchief covering my head. I felt it slipping off.

I tried to get my hand up to hold on to it, but Doctor Askin held my arms. He enfolded me in a crushing hug, and I felt the kerchief sliding down, inching away from the sores it covered, to betray me. The kerchief, as Doctor Askin let go, dropped around my neck, settling on my shoulders like a heavy weight.

With my head exposed to the air, it itched worse than ever.

Quickly my hands flew up to replace the kerchief. I swept it back up in a matter of seconds, trying to cover my head before anyone had a chance to see my scalp.

I wasn't fast enough. Towering over me as he did, Saul had seen it. Doctor Askin had seen it too. They stared down at me.

"Rifka, your head," Saul said.

I pulled the kerchief tightly over my scalp.

Not now, I prayed. They've stamped the papers. Don't let them find out now.

"But Rifka," Saul said. "There's something on your head."

"Take off your kerchief," Doctor Askin ordered.

"Please," I begged in a whisper. "Don't make me take it off."

"Take it off, Rifka," Doctor Askin insisted.

My hands shook as I lifted them to the knot under my chin. I had difficulty untying it. Everyone stared at me, at my trembling hands, at my disloyal kerchief.

"Whatever it is," I said, trying to talk my way out of it, "I'm certain it will go away."

I could delay no longer. The kerchief dropped to my shoulders.

"This isn't going away," said Nurse Bowen. "Here, feel for yourself."

She took my hand and guided it up to the top of my head. I stretched my hand out, expecting to feel the ringworm sores under my fingertips.

But I didn't feel ringworm.

I felt hair!

Not very much. But it was hair. My hair! And it was growing.

• • •

MAMA and Papa are sitting beside me on a bench at Ellis Island. We are waiting for my brother Isaac. I am writing on the paper Nurse Bowen gave to me.

Saul says at home there is a notebook full of paper, a whole empty notebook for me to write in. He bought it for me himself, with his own money. And at home is a pair of brass candlesticks, he said. A pair just like the ones Mama used to own.

Tonight, Saul said, tonight I would give them to her.

On my head is the black velvet hat with the shirring and the light blue lining. My head still itches, but Nurse Bowen said that is normal. That often the scalp prickles when new hair grows in.

Mama's gold locket lies softly between her breasts again, where it belongs. Around my neck is a small Star of David on a silver chain, a gift from Mama and Papa.

"Saul said this is what you would like the most," Mama had said when she gave it to me.

"Saul was right," I said, and I kissed Mama and Papa on their hands, first one and then the other.

My brother Isaac has gone home to Borough Park to bring his car. He said, "Never mind the trouble, my sister Rifka is going to enter America in style."

A clever girl like me, Tovah, how else should I enter America?

I will write you tonight a real letter, a letter I can send. I will wrap up our precious book and send it to you too, so you will know of my journey. I hope you can read all the tiny words squeezed onto the worn pages. I hope they bring to you the comfort they have brought to me. I send you my love, Tovah. At last I send you my love from America.

> *Shalom, my dear cousin,*
> *Rifka*

Connected Readings

from
Land of Promise

Joan Lowery Nixon

ROSE CARNEY snatched up her skirts with one hand and ran as fast as she could down the path that led from the Ellis Island inspection station to the New Jersey ferry as its whistle gave two long, sharp blasts.

Her friend Kristin Swensen and her parents had already joined the line of immigrants who had passed the dreaded physical and mental examinations and would enter the United States through Jersey City, hub of the railroad lines that led to many distant parts of the United States. Muttering to herself, Rose hurried to catch up with the Swensens while at the same time she tried to keep her wicker suitcase from bumping against her legs and throwing her off balance.

Rose was furious with her uncle Jimmy for deserting her at the immigration station. She'd counted on traveling with him to Chicago, where they'd join her father and two older brothers, but Uncle Jimmy had abruptly broken the news that he was staying in New York.

"You're a big girl, almost grown," he'd told her as he tucked a railway ticket into her hands, "and perfectly able to travel to Chicago by yourself."

As Uncle Jimmy disappeared through the door that led to the New York ferries, there'd been no time for Rose to tell him just what she thought. Now, as she rushed toward the ferry, she grumbled through a dozen angry I-should-have-saids.

"I can't believe I have to make the trip to Chicago alone!" she told the Swensens as she tried to catch her breath.

She heard the tremor of fear in her voice and, trying to get herself in hand, silently scolded herself. *You're not a child, Rosie Carney. You were frightened when you left Liverpool for the United States on that great whale of a ship, but you made the voyage without mishap. And there's no reason why you can't join your father in Chicago still in one piece.*

As the ferry chugged away from the dock, Kristin sat down and patted a place for Rose. "You won't be alone," she said with a smile. "Father told me we'll be traveling with you all the way to Chicago."

"How could that be?" Rose asked. "You're going to Minnesota, not Chicago."

"Look at your ticket. It says the Chicago, Milwaukee and St. Paul Railway," Kristin explained, and laughed at Rose's loud sigh of relief.

Rose lowered her voice even though Mr. and Mrs. Swensen had made their way through the crowd of passengers to the rail and were watching the massive, towered, red-and-yellow brick building on Ellis Island recede into the distance. "I can't help worrying about meeting my father again," she confided. "It's been almost four years since he left Ireland, and I was only a girl of twelve. What if he doesn't recognize me?" Rose swallowed hard, then continued, "I confess that even though Ma had an old photograph of him, taken when he was young, sometimes it's hard to remember his face. What if *I* don't recognize *him?*"

"You'll find each other with no trouble," Kristin assured Rose. "Take off your kerchief, and that red hair of yours will be like a beacon light flashing: Here's Rose! Here's Rose!"

Rose couldn't keep from smiling. "I wish that Da could have afforded to bring Ma and my younger sisters to the United States with me. I've never before, in almost sixteen years, been separated from my mother." A little enviously she added, "You and Rebekah are lucky that your families could come to the United States together."

"You said there'd be enough money to send for your mother and sisters in two years. That's not so long," Kristin said, but her voice lacked conviction.

"It *is* a long time," Rose insisted.

Her eyes burned with tears as she pictured Ma, Bridget, and Meggie on the Liverpool docks nearly three weeks before. She fought back the tears, twisting to peer at the receding New York skyline, forcing herself to think of anything else.

"I hope that all goes well for Rebekah and her family," Rose managed. "New York City seems so crowded. I hear it's a terrifying place. I wouldn't want to live there."

"It must be exciting," Kristin said. "I think I'd like to live in a city. Life can be awfully dull on a farm." She gave Rose a careful look. "Chicago's a big city, too. My father said so."

Rose shivered and drew her shawl more closely around her shoulders. "Much like Dublin, I suppose, and I'm not a bit comfortable in Dublin with all its noise and horses and carts and people hurrying along the streets when they aren't packed into buildings like eggs in a crate."

"I think Rebekah will be happy living in New York City," Kristin said, "because she wants an education, and a city has schools."

Rose ached as she thought about Rebekah, the other friend she had made on board the ship. Befriending Kristin and Rebekah had made the dreadful voyage in steerage bearable; although their lives and futures were so different, the girls felt as though they'd been friends for years. Rose hated the fact that they'd had to part.

"Do you really think that one day the three of us will be together again?" Rose asked.

"I *know* we will." Kristin nodded emphatically. "I believe in making things happen."

The ferry bumped against the dock, and many of the passengers snatched up their belongings, pushing and shoving toward the gangplank.

"Stand back! Move aside!" the crew yelled as they slung lines to the dock, then jumped down to swiftly pull from the ship the attached hawsers, dropping their heavy loops around the mushroom-shaped bits that rose from the dock.

Mr. Swensen, who was taller and broader shouldered than most of the other men on board, had no trouble shepherding his family down the short gangplank onto the dock. Kristin reached out a hand and dragged Rose along.

They walked to the nearby railway station, which was crowded with passengers.

"Look at that gentleman with his top hat and gold-tipped cane," Kristin whispered to Rose, but Rose was more interested in the bright posters tacked on the posts and walls throughout the station.

"California—Cornucopia of the World," one of them read. "Room for Millions of Immigrants." Rose continued reading, "43,795,000 Acres of Government Lands Untaken. A Climate for Health and Wealth without Cyclones or Blizzards."

Another touted Texas over the crowded eastern states, and a third poster announced that Kansas was the "Golden Belt Country."

Mr. Swensen, who had gone ahead to inquire about their train, elbowed his way back through the crowd, beaming. "Hear what they say about Minnesota: 'One immense empire of mineral, timbered, and agricultural wealth, waiting only to be occupied.' Was I not right to bring us here?"

Mrs. Swensen nodded yes, but Kristin said, "Pappa, we can't be sure until we arrive and see for ourselves."

Still smiling, Kristin's father answered, "We will soon be on our way to discovering the answer. Come. This way. Our train will leave in less than an hour."

"How long will it take to get to Chicago?" Rose asked.

"Chicago is around eight hundred and fifty miles or so. It will take a little more than two days and nights—we'll arrive the morning of the third day."

Nearly three days! Rose had not thought about where Chicago was located. It would be a long journey. She was again furious with her uncle. She'd left everything up to him. She was even more grateful to be with the Swensens.

"Let's move on now," said Mr. Swensen. Mrs. Swensen and Kristin hurried after him, Rose straggling along in the rear with her heavy suitcase.

Suddenly Rose felt a tug on her suitcase and whirled to see a smiling young man who was trying to pry her fingers from the handle of the case. With his free hand he tipped his cap and said, "I'll carry this for you, miss."

"I thank you, but I can carry the case myself," Rose told him.

The man's grip didn't loosen. "I'm no fool. If you think you've found a way to steal my belongings, then you've made a big mistake," Rose announced.

He tugged, but Rose was faster and kicked with all her strength at his shins. Then she balled her fist and smashed it into the bridge of his nose.

As the man let out a yell and jumped back, he released the suitcase and grabbed at his bleeding nose. Rose clutched her suitcase against her chest and used it as a ram to open a path through the milling passengers as she scurried after her traveling companions who were now up ahead.

Rose and the Swensens entered one of the railway cars for those who had paid lower fares and stowed their belongings and the packages of food they had purchased for the trip under the hard wooden seats. Rose and Kristin huddled together, noses pressed against the window.

Before long the train reached stretches of open country, and the tracks wound through rolling hills, past stands of aspen and pine, birch and maple. Scatterings of small yellow-and-white wildflowers appeared as bright surprises, and the large fields on the occasional farms they passed were pale green with newly sprouted seedlings.

"Look at the size of the farms!" Rose exclaimed. "These must all belong to titled landowners."

"There are no titles in the United States." Kristin giggled. "It's a democracy."

Rose laughed, too. "There's not a farmer in Ireland with more than a dollop of this much land. Only the wealthy English who stole the Irish estates have farms like these."

Kristin raised one eyebrow. "Stole?"

"Stole," Rose said firmly, "along with deroofing our churches, destroying our forests, and killing our game. For years the Irish were not even allowed to go to school, so some of them—like my parents—learned in secrecy to read and write."

"That's terrible!" Kristin exclaimed.

"Terrible—yes! But someday Ireland will be ours again."

"Are you talking about war?"

"May heaven protect us, I hope there'll be no war with its maimings and killings!" Rose shuddered as she said, "A man on the farm next to us was caught in the Clan na Gael bombings in Britain in the eighties. He was left blinded, and his face was so horribly disfigured from his burns that little children run in terror when they see him coming. Ma says that peaceful discussion is the only answer, not violence, and I agree with Ma. My brothers and father talk about rousting the English by force. I love Ireland, but sometimes I'm frightened to think of what might happen."

"You don't have to be frightened here. This is America," Kristin said, and for a moment the two girls were silent, looking out at the farmland.

"In Ireland we lived on a farm," Rose said, and her throat tightened as memories filled her mind. "Our house was small, with a thatched roof, but the peat-burning stove and the fireplace kept it snug and warm. On cold nights Ma would heat bricks in the ashes and wrap them in towels, then tuck them in our beds to warm our toes."

Kristin nodded. "We had foot warmers, too."

"For a while we had three cows—now only one—and I'd lead them down the lane and over the hill to graze by the lake," Rose said. "Any neighbors who were working their crops would straighten and wave, maybe even come over to lean on the fence for a moment to chat." She smiled. "Old Mrs. O'Malley, may she rest in peace, always had a bit of gossip to pass along."

"Our neighbors in Sweden never stopped their work to talk," Kristin said, "but we all met at the Lutheran church each Sunday, and there were dinners and festivals. We had socials at our school, too."

"But no dances, you told us."

"That's right. Our pastor didn't approve. He was very strict, and when he hit the edge of his desk with his stick even the worst boys in class paid attention." She giggled and turned to Rose. "But I liked school. I really did. Did you?"

"Yes," Rose answered. "I went to school at the convent in Drogheda. Sister Rita was probably as strict as your pastor, but she was generous with praise and hugs. She begged us all to go on to higher education when we reached the age of fourteen, but how could we? None of us could afford it. The few secondary schools were in the cities."

"Cities offer so much that people living on farms can't have," Kristin said.

Rose smiled. "I'm the one who'll be living in a city, and you'll be on a farm. It seems as though we'd gladly change places."

Kristin's sigh was her only answer as she pressed her nose against the dusty glass window and stared out at the countryside.

As the train chugged across the state of Pennsylvania and through upper Ohio and Indiana, the hard benches and the constant swaying and lurching were uncomfortable. At each stop passengers would scramble down the steps, eager to move about and stretch sore muscles. Some depots served hot food, but those travelers who ran inside to order complained later that the service was so slow they had barely been served before the whistle on the train blew long blasts to signal its departure.

Rose was content with the chunks of bread, cheese, salted ham, and apples that Mrs. Swensen had packed, gladly paying her share of the cost to Mr. Swensen, even though Kristin muttered embarrassed remarks about it.

Although she was stiff from trying to sleep sitting up on the hard seats, Rose perked up as a porter walked through their car early the third morning and announced, "We've crossed into Illinois. We'll be in Chicago shortly."

Rose and Kristin hurried to the washroom at the end of the car, where they scrubbed their arms and faces in the small basin and brushed their hair.

Rose tied a clean kerchief over her hair and studied her reflection in the mirror. She was no longer a twelve-year-old girl; she was grown, nearly a woman. Da would be surprised at how she had changed. But he would have changed, too. Was his hair still thick and black? His shoulders as broad and strong? She squeezed her eyes shut, trying to picture her father, Peter Carney, as she had last seen him, but she saw only a blur.

The jolting of the train threw her off balance, and she grabbed Kristin for support.

"You look fine," Kristin told Rose. "Now hurry. We want to look out the windows and see as much of Chicago as we can."

They squeezed past the conductor and the people around him who shouted in a variety of languages.

A short, plump woman pushed a card at Rose. Rose read what was printed on the card: *To the Conductor: Please show bearer where to change trains and where to get off, as this person does not speak English. Bearer is bound to Chicago, Illinois.* Underneath was the name of a civic league for immigrants.

Rose smiled and nodded. "We are coming into Chicago," she said slowly.

The woman grasped the one word she understood. "Chicago?" she echoed.

"Yes." Rose nodded and pointed to herself. "Chicago. I'm going to Chicago, too. I'll tell you when we get there."

The woman took her seat, but she kept her eyes on Rose.

As she sat next to Kristin, Rose murmured, "Another good-bye. First Rebekah, and now you."

"We're friends. We'll write," Kristin said emphatically. "We'll see each other again." But tears ran down her cheeks, and she buried her face against Rose's shoulder.

The train began to slow. As Rose held Kristin tightly, she saw that they were passing clusters of buildings, their dark-red brick covered with layers of soot. *Leonard Seed Company, Platt's Oysters* . . . tracks and more tracks . . . open grain cars on sidings . . . until finally the train crawled, ducking under a covered shed, and stopped, its brakes squealing loudly.

The plump woman pecked at Rose's shoulder. "Chicago?" she asked.

"Yes, Chicago," Rose answered. She struggled to her feet and gave Kristin one last hug. "Don't forget to send me your address as soon as you have one."

She shook hands with Mr. Swensen, but Mrs. Swensen cupped Rose's face with her hands and examined it. "You are pale," she said. "Do you feel ill?"

"No," Rose said and took a deep breath. "The truth is I'm more than a bit nervous about seeing my father again."

"Will he be here to meet you?"

"No," Rose said, "but I have his address. I'm certain there'll be

plenty of good-hearted people who will help me find my way."
She wished she felt as brave as her words. Her stomach hurt
and it was hard to breathe, but she realized there was only one
thing to do—leave the train and find her father's home.

Rose hoisted her suitcase and descended the steps of the railway car. From the wooden platform, Rose glanced at the steepled
and gabled dark-brick station toward which the other passengers
were hurrying . She followed them, pushed open a heavy door,
and found herself in a massive, crowded, high-ceilinged room.

Rose looked for the woman who had asked her for help and
was glad to see that she was surrounded by four tall young men
who happily greeted her. When it was Ma's turn to come she'd
get a royal welcome, too.

But there was no one to meet Rose, and standing in the station gawking at the people around her wouldn't accomplish anything. "Please, sir," Rose called to a uniformed man who was
striding past, "could you tell me where I . . ."

"Sorry," he called over his shoulder as he kept going, "Got
some folks waiting for a porter."

Someone jostled her, and Rose staggered off balance. She re-
gained her footing and looked around indignantly, but the person had gone. "Without so much as an apology," Rose muttered
to herself.

She made her way across the room and out the main doors
onto the sidewalk. Carts and buggies passed at a steady clip,
and an electric cable car rattled through the traffic. Draymen
yelled at their horses, cab drivers shouted for passengers, and
the hubbub was deafening.

Dublin was bad, but Chicago in 1902 was worse. Oh, if she
could only go home and be with her mother and little sisters
again!

from
Ellis Island Interviews

Isaac Bashevis Singer

Isaac Bashevis Singer emigrated to the United States from Poland in 1935, at the age of 31. The son and grandson of rabbis, Singer studied at a rabbinical seminary in Warsaw before beginning his career as a writer. He is best known for his stories set in the Jewish ghettoes of Eastern Europe. Singer went on to win many literary awards including the Nobel Prize for Literature and two National Book Awards. He died in 1991.

I WAS brought up in Warsaw . . . which is not very much unlike New York. It is noisy, it is dirty. There is everything which a big city has, all the good sides and all the bad sides. So I wasn't really very much shocked when I came to this country, to New York, because we had the same thing there in a smaller way. But just the same, we all were brought up that America is almost like a different planet, and in a way I was very confused when I came here.

First of all, I did not know English. I hadn't studied any English there, so I was actually mute when I went to a bus or to a trolley car. I didn't know what to say. In addition, things looked to me very different. For example, when I looked into a drugstore and I saw that they served sandwiches there, I was bewildered because for us a drugstore was a most dignified place where one took off one's hat, and the idea that people sit there on little benches, and drink coffee, and smoke, looked to me almost sacrilege. Now, I know, that it was silly because there is nothing special about the drugstore . . .

In fact, so many things looked so different that I thought, in my heart, I will never be able to write about this country. And the truth is, for thirty years, I never dared to write anything about this country, but now I have been here in America longer than I had been in Poland and I would say that I have my deep roots also here. And I have learned, it is true, that I don't write about people born in this country, I write mostly about immigrants, but at least I dare to write about America.

There was anti-Semitism (in Warsaw), but I personally did not have much of this kind of experience, because I always lived among Jewish people, on the Jewish streets. First, I went to the synagogue or to the study house where I studied the Talmud, and there was no anti-Semitism there. Later, I was connected with the Yiddish writers for the Yiddish Writers Club, so although I knew that it existed and I read about it in the newspapers, I personally didn't have any trouble.

However, what you read in the newspapers is very much real, and you know that what happened to another man can the next day happen to you, so we were all afraid, especially in the '30s. Men from a pro-Fascist party, they were almost pro-Nazi, visited Poland, and we Jews knew that Poland was a very dangerous place for us. This was one of the reasons, or perhaps the main reason, why I wanted to get away from there. Also, my brother was here, who was a writer, many years older than I. I considered him my master, my teacher, and I wanted to be together with him.

I came by boat, a French boat called *Champlain.* I was told later that this boat was sunk during the war. It was quite an elegant, beautiful boat. As a matter of fact, the agent from whom I bought the ticket told me that if I would have waited another two weeks I could have gone with the *Normandy,* which made its maiden voyage, and this was considered among many people a great privilege to go on this first trip. But I felt that the ship would not add anything to my value. I came here the first of May 1935. I traveled tourist class, which was good enough for me.

I remember my arrival quite well. A man from the *Jewish Daily Forward* waited for me and also my brother, and they took me in a car. My first impression was New York is a city like all cities. It is not the planet Mars or Venus or Jupiter. When I saw the skyscrapers, I felt there was something unusual, but just the same, the Polish had already tried to build a skyscraper in Warsaw, a lower skyscraper, let's say. It had eighteen floors, but even this was big.

Many immigrants had this kind of feeling that America is so different that they really felt that they were coming into a different world, but I don't have to tell you that the world is actually the same. It only takes time until you learn the language and you get acquainted with people, you realize that human nature is everywhere the same. Although there are many differences, I would say that American people looked to me then, and they look to me now, more kind and more sincere and more ready to help people than the Europeans. But there is also a reason for this, because American people are richer and they are accustomed to immigrants. They are not clannish as the Europeans are, where people have fought for every inch of earth for generations. There are great differences, but there are also many, many things which are common to all people.

The first thing I saw from the ship was the Statue of Liberty, and it always made a great impression on me. Immigrants . . . I even heard about the Statue of Liberty when I was a small boy in Warsaw, when I went to *heder.* They spoke about this because there were many people in our neighborhood who could not read or write, and they had relatives in America, so they came to my mother that she should read their letters. And they all wrote about it, how they came to America, how they saw the Statue of Liberty, and they also wrote about Ellis Island, which they called the Island of Tears, and about all the troubles some of the immigrants had when they came. There was a great fear of this island because people were told that if the doctors find that someone is sick, or they think he is sick, they send him back.

● ● ●

A COUNTRY where the great majority are immigrants is different than a country where people have been living for hundreds of years, but this doesn't mean that the difference makes a country of immigrants worse. It may be even the opposite, because people who come to another country, who are torn out from their homes, learn that things are not just as they thought. When you stay long at home, where you never leave your own country, you have the illusion that everything which happens in your country is hard, this is human nature. If you are accustomed to eating for breakfast, say, a roll and coffee, and you travel and see them eat corn flakes, you think that the world is going to pieces because you see that things can be so different. In a way, traveling is a lesson in tolerance. We learn by traveling and by immigrating. . . .

Ukraine's Troubled History
from The Handbook of the
Former Soviet Union

Michael G. Kort

> *Rifka Nebrot and her family emigrated to the United States in order to escape the persecution of Jews in her hometown of Berdichev in Ukraine, Russia. The following piece examines the turbulent and often violent history of this troubled land.*

THE Ukrainian people, like the Russians and Belarusians, trace their history to the East Slavs and Kievian Rus. However, after Kievian Rus was destroyed by the Mongol invasion of the thirteenth century, Ukraine was carved up by three powers. Although in the west the principality of Galicia-Volhynia maintained its independence for a time, most of today's Ukrainian territory, including Volhynia, eventually fell to Lithuania, which was expanding southeastward from its original core near the Baltic Sea. Poland took Galicia, while Ukraine's eastern fringes became part of the Golden Horde, the state that the Mongols set up on the steppe east of the Black Sea. As power shifted over the next two centuries, the division of Ukraine changed somewhat. Most of Ukraine became part of a unified Polish-Lithuanian state, while its Black Sea coast was seized by a new power in the region: the Ottoman Empire. By the sixteenth century, several pieces of the eastern Ukraine belonged to yet another new and growing power, the principality of Muscovy.

It is this history of being torn at by the great powers that surrounded it that gave Ukraine its name, which means "borderland" in both Russian and Ukrainian. In the mid-seventeenth century, a rebellion against Poland led by a Cossack chieftain named Bogdan Khmelnytsky swept Ukraine. Thousands of Ukrainian peasants rallied to Khmelnytsky's banner, and he succeeded in defeating the Poles. However, this struggle for independence had a dark and ugly side. As they fought the Poles, Khmelnytsky's forces also turned their fury against the region's Jewish population. They murdered about 100,000 people, one of the worst massacres of Jews in history prior to the Holocaust committed by Nazi Germany in the twentieth century.

By the time the period the Ukrainians call the "Ruin" was over, the country was divided among the Russians, Poles, and Ottomans. Gradually the Russian Empire expanded at the expense of the weakening Poles and Ottomans, until it had conquered virtually all of Ukraine by the end of the eighteenth century. Only its western fringe, which was seized by the Austrian Empire, escaped Russian control.

The next important development in Ukrainian history centered around language rather than politics. Modern Ukrainian emerged from several dialects spoken in the region in the fifteenth and sixteenth centuries. The language had an oral tradition of epic poems, folk songs, and folktales. A literary tradition also emerged, consisting largely of works by Ukrainian Orthodox clergy that often were anti-Polish. However, the first great writer of the modern Ukrainian language was Taras Shevchenko (1814–1861). His poems depict Ukrainian rural life and express the poet's love for his native land. Because he advocated Ukrainian independence, Shevchenko was sent into Siberian exile. After his death the tsarist regime intensified its policy of Russification, which included banning Ukrainian-language publications and theatrical productions. However, it was unable to stop the growing nationalist movement, as historians, writers, and poets followed Shevchenko's lead.

In March 1917, for the first time in nearly three centuries, Ukraine received a second chance at independence when the tsarist empire collapsed. At first a council called the Rada asked only for autonomy, but it proclaimed Ukraine's independence when the Bolsheviks seized power. Ukraine again became a battleground, as Bolsheviks, anti-Bolsheviks, and several Ukrainian nationalist factions fought for supremacy. Once again the turmoil left Ukraine divided and under foreign control. By the end of the civil war in 1921, most of Ukraine had been conquered by Bolshevik forces. However, a large swath in the west was in Polish hands, and a few bits and pieces were part of Czechoslovakia and Romania.

Ukraine Under Soviet Rule

SOVIET rule was a catastrophe for Ukraine, as it was for every other state of the former Soviet Union, including Russia. As was the case in the other Soviet republics, the first seven years after the civil war offered a chance for recovery. The Soviet regime in Moscow permitted the Ukrainians to speak and write their language, which led to a genuine cultural revival. Ukrainian peasants were allowed to run their own farms under a moderate program called the New Economic Policy. But bad times lay ahead. In the Biblical story of Joseph in Egypt, seven good years are followed by seven bad years. In the Ukraine in the twentieth century, seven good years were followed by almost sixty bad years.

By 1928, Joseph Stalin was consolidating his personal dictatorship. Supported by Communist Party zealots who were determined to build a new socialist order and prepared to destroy anything that stood in their way, Stalin launched his program of rapid industrialization and collectivization of agriculture. Ukrainian peasants bitterly resisted collectivization, but to no avail. Huge numbers of them were shot or arrested and deported to slave labor camps. At least five million more peasants died in the 1932–1933 famine that accompanied collectivization when the Soviet regime seized most of the food from the farms and left the peasants to starve. Stalin's purges of the 1930s, when millions of people were murdered outright or sent to be worked to death in Soviet slave-labor camps, dealt yet another blow to Ukraine.

The next disaster to hit Ukraine was World War II. The German invasion of the Soviet Union brought massive suffering. The death toll in Ukraine was about six million, of whom one million were Jews murdered as part of the organized Nazi campaign to exterminate the Jewish people. An additional two million Ukrainians were drafted to work as slave laborers for the Nazis. Hundreds of thousands of Ukrainians fought the Nazis as members of the Soviet Red Army and as guerrillas. At the same time, there were Ukrainians who helped the Nazis round up and murder their Jewish neighbors or served as concentration camp guards. In two days and nights in September 1941, 35,000 Jews were shot to death, a pace of murder that not even the Nazis' extermination camps could match. Thousands of them were driven to their place of execution at the Babi Yar ravine outside Kiev through a corridor formed by Ukrainian police.

After the Germans finally were driven from Ukraine and the rest of the Soviet Union, and World War II came to an end, some Ukrainian guerrilla forces resisted the return of Soviet rule. These anti-Soviet rebels were not totally wiped out until 1949. Meanwhile, the extreme western part of Ukraine, which had been held by Poland and Czechoslovakia prior to 1939, was seized by the

Soviet Union in 1945 and annexed to Ukraine. Further territorial growth came in 1954, a year after Stalin's death, when the new Soviet leader, Nikita Khrushchev, detached the Crimean Peninsula from the Russian republic and gave it to Ukraine.

Ukraine remained relatively quiet during the 1950s, but in the 1960s and 1970s both nationalist and democratic movements emerged. The Soviet regime under Leonid Brezhnev reacted with a widespread purge beginning in 1972. Although the purge was not violent, as in the Stalin years, many people lost their jobs, including Ukrainian Communist Party leader Petr Shelest. He was replaced by Vladimir Shcherbitsky, a hard-line, dictatorial bureaucrat who ran Ukraine with an iron hand for his bosses in Moscow. However, not even Shcherbitsky could crush the unrest in Ukraine. Underground publications by intellectuals and dozens of strikes by workers were proof that discontent remained beneath the surface and would not disappear.

The Gorbachev Era

ALTHOUGH the emergence of Mikhail Gorbachev immediately brought a breath of fresh air to the stagnant atmosphere in the Kremlin in Moscow, it still took months for his policies of glasnost and perestroika to build up any steam. Glasnost, which means openness, referred to allowing the Soviet people more access to information and permitting them an expanded freedom to express themselves. Perestroika originally referred to a restructuring of the Russian economy but soon came to refer to the entire program of reform. The process was particularly slow in Ukraine, where Shcherbitsky was one of the most effective Communist Party bosses standing against reform. Most of the Brezhnev-era policies against dissidents and others who wanted to loosen the party's hold on the life of the people remained in place.

Then came Chernobyl. On April 26, 1986, an explosion tore apart one of the nuclear reactors at the Chernobyl nuclear power plant, not far from Kiev. Deadly radioactive particles were blown into the atmosphere and then began silently to rain down on the unsuspecting inhabitants near the disaster site. To the nuclear disaster was added a political one, as Soviet authorities failed to inform the people of what had happened, and in fact did not admit to the disaster until radioactivity was detected in Western Europe. Many of the heroic men who stopped the fire caused by the explosion from reaching the other nuclear reactors at Chernobyl later died from radioactive poisoning because they lacked protective clothing. It took days before people living near the extreme danger zone finally were evacuated. The Soviet government was humiliated both by the explosion and by its failure to respond appropriately.

The Chernobyl disaster had two immediate consequences. It spurred Gorbachev to increase the pace of his reforms across the Soviet Union, and, in Ukraine, it increased unrest against Shcherbitsky's authoritarian rule. A major step took place in November 1988 with the founding of the Ukrainian People's Movement for Restructuring (Rukh). Although Rukh's stated goal was to support reform within the Soviet structure, it soon began to advocate what it vaguely called "sovereignty." Eventually it called for outright independence. By 1989, a broad movement composed of many groups demanding change had developed. It included environmentalists, religious groups, and, perhaps most importantly, well organized and militant miners in the Donbass region, who organized strikes that threatened to bring the Ukrainian economy to its knees. This agitation led to Shcherbitsky's downfall in September, but the turmoil continued. In July 1990, after local elections saw non-Communists win more than 35 percent of the seats in the Ukrainian parliament, Ukraine declared its sovereignty. Shortly thereafter, the parliament elected a former Communist leader named Leonid Kravchuk as its chairman.

During late 1990 and into 1991, Ukrainian leaders consistently opposed Gorbachev's efforts to hold the country together until the unsuccessful August coup against him shattered the last vestiges of Soviet power. On August 24, just three days after the coup against Gorbachev collapsed, the Ukrainian parliament declared the country's independence. Barely three months after that, on December 1, Ukrainian voters went to the polls and voted overwhelmingly for independence, effectively destroying Gorbachev's last desperate attempt to preserve the Soviet Union. On the same day, the voters chose Leonid Kravchuk to be the new republic's first president. On December 31, the Soviet Union was dissolved, making Ukraine's independence an established fact.

Twice before—in the mid-seventeenth and early twentieth centuries—Ukraine had reached for independence. But both attempts occurred during raging storms of rebellion and war, and when those winds of war finally died down, Ukraine found itself once again under foreign control. In 1991, whatever other troubles it faced, Ukraine was at peace, and its neighbors, particularly Russia, were in no position to challenge its independence.

Independent Ukraine

UKRAINE began the first era of independence in its history beset by many problems. Soviet policies that emphasized industrial growth over all else had made the country an environmental disaster area. Many of Ukraine's rivers, including the Dnieper, are polluted by industrial wastes and radioactive materials. The air in many cities is heavily polluted by industrial waste from chemical and metallurgical factories. Uranium mining has given the country some of the highest cancer rates in the world. Erosion and the overuse of chemicals have ruined millions of acres of farmland. And always there will be Chernobyl. In 1989 a young mother from a farming village near Chernobyl spoke to a reporter about how pollution was ruining her life and the lives of her children. Although she was speaking about her own village, her poignant words applied to millions of people throughout Ukraine whose health was endangered by environmental pollution:

> I was raised [on this land], it reared my children. And we eat virtually everything that is produced on it because it is impossible to obtain anything else. . . . So we eat everything that the earth produces, even though it has been contaminated. . . . I have four children and they are all sick. Commission after commission visits here, but to no avail. My heart bursts with grief when I see the sick children. We are hostages. We have no opportunity to leave, yet it is impossible to live here.

Seventy years of Soviet communism also left much of Ukraine's population without conveniences that are considered necessities in the industrialized world. Perhaps worst off were the villages and farms, where about one third of the people live. Rural areas were ignored or exploited for many years while the Soviets focused on industrial development. As Ukraine began its independent life, only one third of its villages had medical facilities, and most of those were minimal. Most lacked even the most basic cultural facilities, such as a hall where movies could be shown. The majority of Ukraine's villages lacked running water, and only 5 percent were linked to gas lines.

In addition, as elsewhere in the former Soviet Union, Ukraine had no tradition of democratic government. Its president, Leonid Kravchuk, was a former Communist Party leader who managed to overhaul his political identity and suddenly emerge as a new-born Ukrainian nationalist just as the Soviet Union was collapsing. As president, Kravchuk initially maintained his popularity by stressing his determination to strengthen Ukraine and ensure its independence from Russia. The disputes with Russia over Ukraine's nuclear arms, the Crimea, and the former Soviet Union's Black Sea naval fleet bolstered Kravchuk's popularity, but did little to make life better for the average citizen. In November 1992, to further separate his country from its giant neighbor, Kravchuk replaced the Russian ruble with a new Ukrainian currency, another step that met with popular approval.

However, Kravchuk took few steps toward real economic reform; in particular, he did not move Ukraine toward building a free-enterprise system. He often responded to those who disagreed with him with threats, like the Soviet official he once was, rather than like the democratic president he was supposed to be. One member of parliament summed up his concern about the president's priorities, which focused on Ukrainian independence at the expense of almost everything else:

> We reject the notion that one must concentrate on first building the state, and that democracy is of secondary importance. With that attitude, God knows what kind of state—authoritarian, even fascist—we may end up with.

Meanwhile, in the wake of Kravchuk's inaction, the Ukrainian economy continued the decline that began during the Gorbachev era. Between 1990 and 1994, economic output dropped by 50 percent. Ukraine's new currency, introduced in late 1991, was eroded by inflation that peaked in 1993 at an annual rate of 4,735 percent. That year coal miners in the Donbass region in the eastern part of the country, many of whom were ethnic Russians, were on strike. Ordinary people found it increasingly difficult to pay for basic food necessities. As one economist put it: "It would not be an exaggeration to call the situation catastrophic. Those who call it a crisis are dangerous optimists."

Ukraine also was plagued by ethnic conflicts that threatened its unity. The most dangerous situation was in Crimea, an autonomous republic where the overwhelming majority of the population was ethnic Russian and where sentiment for secession from Ukraine and reunion with Russia was strong. In January 1994, Crimean voters elected separatist Yury Meshkov as their republic's president. This began a tug-of-war between Crimea's Russian community and the central government in Kiev that lasted until March 1995, when the Ukrainian parliament abolished Crimea's constitution and dissolved its post of president.

Despite its many problems, in March 1994, Ukraine held elections to its 450-member parliament, called the Supreme Rada. The leading vote-getter was the reorganized Ukrainian Communist Party, which won about a third of the seats. Although they voted for a party that opposed market reforms in March, in July Ukrainian voters chose Leonid Kuchma, a committed economic reformer, as president over Kravchuk. His program of economic reform, which included privatization of state-owned businesses, immediately caused tension with the Rada and its strong Communist bloc. Nonetheless, in late 1994, Kuchma was able to mobilize enough public support to get the Rada to go along with his economic program. The Rada also voted him new powers to carry out his reforms. In addition, Kuchma took the lead in persuading the Rada to approve the nuclear Non-Proliferation Treaty (NPT), under which Ukraine agreed not to acquire nuclear arms. The NPT was the last of the treaties that Ukraine had to approve to clear the way for further United States-Russian nuclear-arms reductions.

Kuchma began implementing his economic reform program in 1995. He was helped with aid from several international organizations, including the International Monetary Fund. At the same time, Kuchma appeared to change his position regarding Russia. During the election campaign he supported closer ties with Russia, and was elected on the strength of strong support from Ukraine's ethnic Russian community. By 1995, however, he was speaking about "Ukraine's return to Europe" and stressing that he did not intend for Ukraine to become "a vassal of Russia."

During 1996, Ukraine took some important steps forward. Early in June the government announced that it had shipped the last of Ukraine's nuclear warheads to Russia for destruction there. At a ceremony at a missile base now empty of weapons, officials from Ukraine, Russia, and the United States scattered sunflower seeds to mark the region's return to growing life-sustaining crops instead of housing instruments of death. At the end of the month the Supreme Rada, after months of opposition from Communist lawmakers, finally adopted Ukraine's first post-Soviet constitution.

Ukraine was the last country of the former Soviet Union to adopt a new constitution. The document contained several compromises. It provides for a strong presidency, as President

Kuchma demanded, but also for a single-chamber legislature, which Kuchma's opponents in parliament wanted. Ukrainian is the official state language, but minorities such as Russians and Crimean Tatars have the right to use and be educated in their own languages. On some issues, such as the right to own private property, Ukraine's new constitution is vague, and when it was adopted parts were not even written down. Yet its adoption was a major step toward making Ukraine what Kuchma called a "predictable country." In September, Ukraine's economy became more predictable when the government introduced a new currency, the *hryvna*. It replaced the currency introduced shortly after independence, which had been severely devalued by five years of inflation.

Ukraine is a country with great potential that remains beset by instability. During 1996 its prime minister, Pavlo Lazarenko, barely escaped death in an assassination attempt when a remote-controlled bomb exploded near his car. The challenge ahead is to make independence work to better the lives for the majority of the Ukrainian people.

from
Such a Life

Edith LaZebnik

*Only sixteen at the time she emigrated alone to the United
States, Edith LaZebnik risked her life to escape the dangers
faced by Polish Jews. LaZebnik was one of millions who
came to the United States in search of the freedom she was
denied amidst the poverty and pogroms of Eastern Europe.
Here she describes parts of her journey.*

WE were eight girls going to Warsaw on the train. The agent
brought us to a hotel, stinking from the street from fish, like a bar-
racks where soldiers stay. At night we slept on the floor and the
mice bit our feet. Food? We couldn't eat. It was like garbage. Three
weeks we suffered before the agent came back. He told us now to
go on the train, but it was far from the city. We had to walk with
our heavy bundles almost a whole day until we came to the train.
Then it took us away, and it stopped in a little town. The agent
said we had to go to a small house far away from the town. Oy, we
walked nearly a whole day again. We had to wait till night the next
day, sitting on the floor and sleeping, eating only bread and tea.
Night came. It was very dark, and we were eighty people and some
little children. One woman was going to her husband, with a one-
year-old child. When he went to America, she was pregnant.

Finally, after two days, the agent came and led us out in the
dark. On the way there were Russian soldiers. The agent paid
them not to look at us. We would lie on the grass in a lot of hay,
and then the agent would take us from one soldier to the next.
We went that way for fifteen miles. We had no more strength
and we all dropped to the ground. If they caught us, we would
get shot or they would kill the soldiers. So no one said a word.
Then it started to rain. Near me was a woman with a child in
her arms, crying. A soldier ran quickly to her and told her she
had to keep the baby quiet. But the rain got worse and the baby
cried harder. The soldier said, "If you don't keep the baby quiet,
I'll have to kill you, or else everybody will be killed."

When I heard that, I was like a dead person, and I told her to
give me the child. I rocked the baby and sang a nice song.

"Shah, shah," I said softly, and the baby fell asleep. Then I told the mother I couldn't carry the baby anymore, I was so tired. So the mother took the baby again, but it cried. The mother covered its mouth to keep it quiet and she prayed, "God, oy, God, don't let my child die." She wrapped up the baby so tight no one could hear if it cried.

Then a river came and we had to cross up to our waists. One soldier saw that I was going to fall, and he took me on his back. I weighed ninety pounds then. I thanked him and he carried me until daylight. When we came out of the river, wet and without strength, and no sleep or food, we were over the border, but we thought we had still more to go.

Then we saw big wagons with a lot of straw, each one with four horses. By every wagon a man was standing, and we were all scared. It rained so hard we couldn't walk. I felt sick and I cried from the cold. All of a sudden two soldiers came onto the road. They laughed at how we were standing, wet and shaking. The agent whispered quickly we should put together kupkes, like quarters, and give to them. We did and they went away. Then he told us to get into the wagons. "Now you're in Germany," he said. "Go in good health." Him we never saw again.

We traveled a half day till we came to a little town where they took us into a big house with one big room for women and children, and a separate one for men. We waited for them to take us by train to Berlin and then to Bremen, where the ship was. Three weeks we waited. I had brought a little bit to eat, my mother had put it in. But it was all gone. One week they didn't give us food. By me was sewn in my coat fifty rubles. When you came to America, you had to show money. That's the way it was then. I was scared to take out some rubles to buy food. After two days without eating, I took out five rubles.

Finally, like we were dead, they took us out of the house and we went by train to Berlin. There, they put one thousand immigrants in a big place with a lot of bunks for sleeping. One man was standing with a whip whirling over his head like you drive cattle. He hurt me with the whip and it got dark in my eyes, and I cried. A young man ran over and hit him in the face and yelled at him, "We are people!" And everybody started to yell, "We are people!"

In Bremen we had to stay two more weeks till the boat left. I didn't have what to eat. In the bunk near me was a Polish woman. "Come with me and we'll eat together," she said. But I couldn't, I didn't have any more money. I didn't want to write home because if they sent money, it wouldn't come in time. And that's the way we both lay and talked. She told me she was there for five weeks, from Warsaw she came. She said she had some money and that she would buy me every day a bowl soup. That's the way I ate. The Polish woman said when we get to America we would see each other and I would pay her. She couldn't go yet because she had to heal her eyes. I never saw her again.

Finally came the time we should go and we went to the boat. A little boat we took to get to the big boat. *Bremen* they called it. It was in the Russian war with Turkey, a very old ship. It danced on the water like a ballerina. Everybody got sick right away. The bread was so hard we used to throw it in the ocean. We lay in the bottom of the boat and rats jumped over us as we screamed. There was a big storm and the boat was crying like an old woman, oy, in her bones, and everybody was yelling that pretty soon the boat was going to break, and the sailors were running up and down, and water came in through the bottom.

That's the way it was on the ocean for thirty-two days. We arrived in America on Sunday. Everybody was standing on one side of the boat, so they told us we had to move around or the boat would tip over. Like a hand held toward us, America was waving. Everybody was waving back. Hello, hello, here we are.

Mighty Woman With a Torch

Nancy Smiler Levinson

A DENSE, misty fog hovered over New York Harbor, but the officials on Bedloe's Island refused to let the gloomy weather interfere with their ceremony. No matter that the Statue of Liberty, still partly veiled, could barely be seen in the fog. The enormous monument had been in the making for fifteen years, and a great many people had long awaited this momentous occasion.

The statue was a gift to the United States from France, which so admired American democracy and wished to seal the friendship between the two countries. France had helped America win its fight for independence from England a century earlier, and America had become a shining example of liberty to the world. Many Frenchmen had tired of wars and revolutions and leadership by despotic emperors in their own country. By presenting a gift symbolizing liberty, they also hoped to give a message to their rulers, expressing their own desire for democracy.

One of those hopeful Frenchmen was a renowned sculptor named Frédéric Auguste Bartholdi. He had enthusiastically accepted the idea of building such a statue when it was suggested by a friend. Auguste always favored massive statuary, but this would be greater than anything he had ever done. The agreement between the two countries had held that France would build the statue, while America would erect the pedestal large enough and grand enough to support it.

After so many years of work, faced with more hurdles than he cared to recall, Auguste had finally accomplished his mission.

Now on this day, October 28, 1886, the handsome, bearded sculptor joined the throngs of people gathering for the dedication ceremony. First the officials, the bands and armed forces units, the groups of schoolchildren, and the numerous patriotic societies—numbering twenty thousand people in all—made their way along a five-mile parade route in lower New York City. The parade took so long, the lunch planned for the officials had to be canceled.

Then, at last, the American and French dignitaries embarked in boats that took them from the Battery across to the tiny island. Immediately harbor festivities began with a display of three hundred water vessels and the sounds of booming cannons and shrill steam whistles. Bands played "Hail Columbia," "Yankee

Doodle," and the French national anthem, "La Marseillaise."

The dignitaries, including President Grover Cleveland, and even several French citizens from Auguste's distant hometown of Colmar, stepped onto the platform that had been constructed especially for the ceremony.

Auguste took a different place, however. He climbed up three hundred feet above the crowd and perched himself in the torch that Miss Liberty majestically held high overhead. There he grasped a rope tied to a three-colored sheet that was draped over the top of the statue. He was to await a signal from a teenage boy selected to let Auguste know when to pull the rope for the unveiling.

The first speaker was a clergyman, who read a prayer. He was followed by several more speakers. Then Senator William M. Evarts, a former secretary of state, stood to say a few well-chosen words. But when he paused in the middle to take a breath, the young boy mistook the pause for the end of his speech. Quickly and eagerly he signaled up to the torch. On cue, Auguste yanked the rope, and the large sheet fell away. There, at last, stood the magnificent copper monument—the woman holding the torch in her right hand and the Declaration of Independence in the other—entitled by the sculptor, Liberty Enlightening the World.

The cheers and shouts, flag waving, and hat tossing at the sight of such an extraordinary work of art were so exuberant that Senator Evarts gave up trying to finish his speech. All he could do was return to his chair. The excitement and clamor continued for such a long time that President Cleveland's words officially accepting the gift on behalf of the American people were barely audible. Yet, he spoke: "We will not forget that Liberty has made here her home, nor shall her chosen altar be neglected . . . a stream of light shall pierce the darkness of ignorance and man's oppression until Liberty enlightens the world."

By then it had begun to drizzle, causing the fireworks display to be postponed until another day. At five o'clock the crowd dispersed to find shelter from the rain and to hurry home and dress for a scheduled banquet.

The list of those who had been invited to the ceremony was lengthy. Of course, many important people were overlooked. But there was one person in particular who was missing that day. Her name was Emma Lazarus.

There was more than one reason Emma was not there to celebrate. First, women were never included in such affairs. Only two were present, Auguste's wife, Jeanne-Emilie, and the wife of one American official. The explanation given was that women might be hurt in the rush of the crowd. Many women were fighting for equal rights at the time, and the suffrage movement calling for the right of women to vote was growing stronger year by year, but it was still a world controlled by men.

Another reason Emma was not invited was that she did not figure importantly in the story of the Statue of Liberty at the time of its unveiling.

That was not to come until later. True, she had written a sonnet about the statue in which she referred to it as "Mother of Exiles." To her it was a symbol welcoming weary immigrants to a country that would allow them to live and worship freely. Her sonnet was entitled "The New Colossus," and it had been written three years earlier, at the urging of Senator Evarts, for an auction to raise money for the pedestal building fund. But "The New Colossus" was printed in a portfolio with other contributors' works, sold to the highest bidder, and forgotten for the time being.

No one at the auction or the dedication ceremony could know the fate of Emma Lazarus's inspired work, but her words were to become immortal and would stir the hearts of all who read them, whether born on American soil or recently come with hopes and dreams to the promised golden land.

No one knew then that part of her verse would be engraved on a plaque to be placed inside the statue's pedestal.

> "Give me your tired, your poor,
> Your huddled masses yearning to breathe free,
> The wretched refuse of your teeming shore.
> Send these, the homeless, tempest-tost to me,
> I lift my lamp beside the golden door!"

But once these words were emblazoned for all to read, they were to give a deeper and more significant meaning to the statue than it had at the start. Not only did the statue celebrate the ideal of liberty, but it became the world's greatest symbol of freedom and hope. For immigrants, Miss Liberty was their first sight of the new land.

During her lifetime Emma, too, was to grow and change, to become a more deeply fulfilled and enriched person than she imagined possible. Even though she was not an exile from another country, she had traveled a long road. Like the woman with the torch, Emma held her own lamp in hand while searching along the path that ultimately led her to become a poet, a humanist, and a patriot.

Prose and Poetry

Alexander Pushkin

Translated by Walter Arndt

Why, writer, toil with plodding prose?
Give me whatever thought you chose:
To pointed sharpness I will edge it.
With wingèd meters will I fledge it,
Will fit it to the tautened thew,
And bending my obedient bow,
Will send it flashing far and true,
And woe betide our common foe!

A Nation of Nations
from A Nation of Immigrants

John F. Kennedy

Only two generations removed from an immigrant himself, John F. Kennedy believed deeply in improving the immigration policies of the United States. His book, A Nation of Immigrants, *was designed to increase awareness of the great contributions immigrants have made to American life. Kennedy hoped this book would garner support for the immigration reform laws he wished to enact.*

ON May 11, 1831, Alexis de Tocqueville, a young French aristocrat, disembarked in the bustling harbor of New York City. He had crossed the ocean to try to understand the implications for European civilization of the new experiment in democracy on the far side of the Atlantic. In the next nine months, Tocqueville and his friend Gustave de Beaumont traveled the length and breadth of the eastern half of the continent—from Boston to Green Bay and from New Orleans to Quebec—in search of the essence of American life.

Tocqueville was fascinated by what he saw. He marveled at the energy of the people who were building the new nation. He admired many of the new political institutions and ideals. And he was impressed most of all by the spirit of equality that pervaded the life and customs of the people. Though he had reservations about some of the expressions of this spirit, he could discern its workings in every aspect of American society—in politics, business, personal relations, culture, thought. This commitment to equality was in striking contrast to the class-ridden society of Europe. Yet Tocqueville believed "the democratic revolution" to be irresistible.

"Balanced between the past and the future," as he wrote of himself, "with no natural instinctive attraction toward either, I could without effort quietly contemplate each side of the question." On his return to France, Tocqueville delivered his dispassionate and penetrating judgment of the American experiment in his great work *Democracy in America.* No one, before or since,

123

has written about the United States with such insight. And, in discussing the successive waves of immigration from England, France, Spain and other European countries, Tocqueville identified a central factor in the American democratic faith:

> All these European colonies contained the elements, if not the development, of a complete democracy. Two causes led to this result. It may be said that on leaving the mother country the emigrants had, in general, no notion of superiority one over another. The happy and powerful do not go into exile, and there are no surer guarantees of equality among men than poverty and misfortune.

To show the power of the equalitarian spirit in America, Tocqueville added: "It happened, however, on several occasions, that persons of rank were driven to America by political and religious quarrels. Laws were made to establish a gradation of ranks; but it was soon found that the soil of America was opposed to a territorial aristocracy."

What Alexis de Tocqueville saw in America was a society of immigrants, each of whom had begun life anew, on an equal footing. This was the secret of America: a nation of people with the fresh memory of old traditions who dared to explore new frontiers, people eager to build lives for themselves in a spacious society that did not restrict their freedom of choice and action.

Since 1607, when the first English settlers reached the New World, over 42 million people have migrated to the United States. This represents the largest migration of people in all recorded history. It is two and a half times the total number of people now living in Arizona, Arkansas, Colorado, Delaware, Idaho, Kansas, Maine, Montana, Nevada, New Hampshire, New Mexico, North Dakota, Oregon, Rhode Island, South Dakota, Utah, Vermont and Wyoming.

Another way of indicating the importance of immigration to America is to point out that every American who ever lived, with the exception of one group, was either an immigrant himself or a descendant of immigrants.

The exception? Will Rogers, part Cherokee Indian, said that his ancestors were at the dock to meet the *Mayflower*. And some anthropologists believe that the Indians themselves were immigrants from another continent who displaced the original Americans—the aborigines.

In just over 350 years, a nation of nearly 200 million people has grown up, populated almost entirely by persons who either came from other lands or whose forefathers came from other lands. As President Franklin D. Roosevelt reminded a convention of the Daughters of the American Revolution, "Remember, remember always, that all of us, and you and I especially, are descended from immigrants and revolutionists."

Any great social movement leaves its mark, and the massive migration of peoples to the New World was no exception to this rule. The interaction of disparate cultures, the vehemence of the ideals that led the immigrants here, the opportunity offered by a new life, all gave America a flavor and a character that make it as unmistakable and as remarkable to people today as it was to Alexis de Tocqueville in the early part of the nineteenth century. The contribution of immigrants can be seen in every aspect of our national life. We see it in religion, in politics, in business, in the arts, in education, even in athletics and in entertainment. There is no part of our nation that has not been touched by our immigrant background. Everywhere immigrants have enriched and strengthened the fabric of American life. As Walt Whitman said,

> These States are the amplest poem,
> Here is not merely a nation but
>   a teeming Nation of nations.

To know America, then, it is necessary to understand this peculiarly American social revolution. It is necessary to know why over 42 million people gave up their settled lives to start anew in a strange land. We must know how they met the new land and how it met them, and, most important, we must know what these things mean for our present and for our future.

from

By Blue Ontario's Shore

Walt Whitman

These States are the amplest poem,
Here is not merely a nation but a teeming Nation of nations,
Here the doings of men correspond with the broadcast
    doings of the day and night,
Here is what moves in magnificent masses careless of
    particulars,
Here are the roughs, beards, friendliness, combativeness,
    the soul loves,
Here the flowing trains, here the crowds, equality, diversity,
    the soul loves.

from
Hide and Seek

Ida Vos

Would You Like a Star, Too?

TODAY for the first time Rachel must go to school with a yellow star on her coat, a big yellow star, with the word *Jew* written in the middle of it. Thus everyone can see that she is Jewish. The Germans have ordered the wearing of the star, and Rachel finds it horrible.

All her mother did yesterday evening was sew stars on their clothing. "I see stars," Mother said, and they even had to laugh about it.

"I'll take you to the tram," says Papa. "Come on, hurry up, otherwise you'll be late for school."

They put their coats on. How big the star is. Esther's star is even bigger than Rachel's. "It looks that way because Esther has such a small body," their father explains. "That's why her star seems larger."

When they arrive at the tram stop they see many other people with stars on, grown-up people and little people. "All Jews," an old man says. "Yesterday I did not know they were Jews, although I suspected they were."

"You must hold your schoolbag under your arm as you usually do, not against your star," Father admonishes her.

Rachel blushes. Father saw that she was trying to hide her star.

"It's difficult, but if you don't hide your star now, you'll get over the embarrassment more quickly. When the war is over, we'll make a huge fire and we'll throw all the stars of the whole world into it."

"Boy, will that stink!" Rachel exclaims.

"It stinks right now," Leo says. "I smelled the star when I put my coat on."

"Children, here comes the tram," Father calls.

The moment has come. For the first time Rachel will have to go on the tram with that horrible star.

"Come in!" the driver of the tram calls out to them. "It really is springtime in my tram now. All these children with yellow daffodils on their coats. I wish I could wear one."

When they are all inside, many people begin to clap, just as an audience does at the end of a play. Rachel does not understand. A man nudges her. "Bow, the clapping is for you, for your stars."

Rachel does not dare to move. What is that? Are the people clapping for that big yellow star?

The children look at one another. "They are clapping for us," Leo says, and he begins to bow. "Thank you, people. Thank you very much."

A few people do not clap, but look straight ahead instead. Leo approaches one of those people. "Ma'am, would you like a star, too? Tomorrow I'll bring you one. Would you like a star, too, mister?"

"Go away, you little Jew boy," the man replies, and to the woman sitting next to him he says, "You can't cut them down to size. Not the big Jews and not the little ones, either."

Going into Hiding

"THIS is Mrs. Helsloot," says Mother. "She has come to take you. You are going into hiding."

"Going into hiding?" Rachel doesn't know what her mother means. "I'm not going with her," she replies.

"My dear, you must."

"Why haven't Papa and you told us? And what does 'going into hiding' mean?" Rachel asks.

"Going into hiding is this: You hide from the Germans," her mother explains. "It is becoming too dangerous to wait here at home until they come get us. Go along. Esther and you will sleep one night at Mrs. Helsloot's. Tomorrow she will bring you to a village nearby. Papa and I will be there, too. Come, dear, get your scooter and go along." Mother says it in such a special way that Rachel has to listen.

"Remember your scooter," says Mrs. Helsloot. "It is for Anke. You can't use it for the time being, anyway."

"Who is Anke?" asks Rachel.

"She is my little daughter. You'll see her when we're home," Mrs. Helsloot answers.

"Where are we going?" asks Esther.

"I can't tell you," says Mrs. Helsloot. "Imagine that the Germans should arrest us and ask you where you're going. It really is better that you don't know."

Rachel doesn't understand a single thing that Mrs. Helsloot says. After all, it has happened so suddenly.

"Go now." Mother gives Rachel a kiss. "I'll give your love to Papa later. Tomorrow we'll see each other again."

Rachel kisses her mother and they go. She and Esther are on the scooter, and Mrs. Helsloot is walking next to them.

A German flag is hanging from the house on the corner. Under the flag two children are busily eating. It is Lotte and Elly. They are celebrating Hitler's birthday.

"Tomorrow is Hitler's birthday," Lotte said yesterday. "We are going to eat delicious cakes and you're not getting any."

"Keep going! Don't look back!" calls Mrs. Helsloot.

After ten minutes they are walking in a street where they have never been before. "Stand still. Something important is going to happen now," says Mrs. Helsloot.

The woman reaches into her coat pocket. She takes out a scissors and goes toward Esther and Rachel with it.

Rachel feels her star being pulled. She feels Mrs. Helsloot cutting threads. "Don't!" she cries out. "We're not allowed to walk outside without a star. We'll be picked up then." She wants to stop Mrs. Helsloot, but the woman is holding her hand.

"Rachel, from now on you must do what I say," Mrs. Helsloot informs her, "at least if you don't want to be picked up. You're not allowed to walk about *with* a star now."

Mrs. Helsloot continues cutting. With one more pull she has the yellow patch in her hand. They are standing by a sewer. The star disappears into it. Now it is Esther's turn. Esther doesn't mind it so much. Quietly she lets Mrs. Helsloot go about her work.

"Come, children, we'll go on."

The girls step on the scooter again. Esther is standing in front, Rachel in back.

"Goodness!" exclaims Mrs. Helsloot, and she puts a hand over her mouth. "Look at that, Rachel!" The woman points to her coat, where the star was. "You can see exactly where that rotten star was. The rest of your coat is lighter blue than the place where your star was. Esther, make sure that your head remains in front of Rachel's chest."

Rachel is terrified. Her hands are sweaty and her heart is beating in her throat. She wants to go home to Papa and Mama. She does *not* want to go into hiding at all. Imagine that some Germans should come and see that blue patch.

"Heinz," one German would say to another. "This child has taken off her star, and that's not allowed. We'll arrest her."

After they have been walking for fifteen minutes, Mrs. Helsloot says: "Here we are. Go inside quickly."

They come into a house where three girls and a man are sitting at a table. "This is my husband and these are my children," Mrs. Helsloot says.

"Hello, Mr. Helsloot." Rachel and Esther shake hands with Mrs. Helsloot's husband.

"Take your coat off," says the man. "My God, Tine, how did you dare to walk so with that child? She has a star on, a blue one."

"I know that," Mrs. Helsloot explains to her husband. "Luckily it went all right. I'll try to bleach that blue star this evening. I'll get that imprint out."

"I hope so," says Mr. Helsloot. He turns to Rachel and Esther. "Would you like a sandwich? Mmm, a hearty sandwich with brown bread and bacon." Bacon? Rachel is already becoming sick just hearing the word *bacon.* Doesn't that man know that Jewish children may not eat bacon?

"Pardon me," Mr. Helsloot apologizes. "I hadn't thought about it. You don't eat pork."

In the evening Mrs. Helsloot brings them to bed. "Sleep tight," she says. "Tomorrow I'll take you to your parents. We'll go on the tram to Delft, and what happens after that you'll see for yourself."

"We haven't been *allowed* to take a tram for a long time," Rachel wants to say, but she sighs and holds her tongue. She is terribly tired from everything.

"I'm going to try to bleach your coat now. Then when we go tomorrow you'll have no star on it—no yellow one and no blue one. Good night."

Each girl receives a kiss from Mrs. Helsloot. "That's nice," Rachel thinks.

The sisters crawl close to each other. It is pleasant to be together in one bed. At home they sleep in separate beds.

"Where are we now?" whispers Esther.

"Wait," Rachel whispers back. "I'll look." Very quietly she gets out of bed. She opens the curtain. On the other side of the street is a little sign with a street name on it. "All . . . ar . . . I can't read it very well."

"Wait, I'll turn the light on," says Esther, and she pulls the little string hanging above the bed.

"Don't! You must never do that again. When you're in hiding you must never turn the light on when the curtains are open. And the curtains—those must never, never be open, for no one must see you!"

Mrs. Helsloot is standing in the room. "You just have to get used to it," she continues. "It will be hard. Don't be so foolish anymore, all right?"

"No, Mrs. Helsloot," the girls say at the same time.

"It is difficult with your coat, but it probably will work," Mrs. Helsloot says.

"And if it doesn't?" Rachel asks her.

"Then you'll have to put that coat on anyway," the woman tells her. "You'll just hold a book in the place where your star was."

Rachel can't sleep. Esther is breathing very quietly next to her. She is sleeping.

Rachel thinks about tomorrow. Perhaps she will have to go outside without a star and yet with a star. How difficult everything is today.

The door opens very softly.

Mrs. Helsloot is standing in front of the bed. "It worked," she whispers. "No one can see that you have had a star on your coat. Sleep well. Good night."

"Good night, Mrs. Helsloot." Rachel sighs. "And give my regards to your husband."

Foreboding

Alexander Pushkin

Translated by Walter Arndt

Once again there hang beclouded
My horizons, dark with rain;
Envious Fate, in malice shrouded,
Lies in wait for me again.
Will I find the strength to treat it
With disdain and, head unbowed,
Go with fortitude to meet it
As I did when young and proud?

Calmly, though my sails are riven,
I await what lies in store;
Once again I may be driven
Safely to a placid shore.
But foreboding, I confess it,
Brings me parting's fearful knell;
To your hand I fly to press it,
Angel, for a last farewell.

Angel meek and undefiant,
Gently whisper me good-bye,
Mourn: your loving gaze compliant,
Cast it down or raise it high.
In your heart enshrined forever,
I shall not grow faint or old:
Shall be young in hope, and never
Aught but gay and proud and bold.

World Migration in the 1990s
from Immigration

Tricia Andryszewski

IMMIGRANTS coming to America are part of a much larger worldwide pool of migrants (people who have left their homelands). The number of migrants, their reasons for migrating, and their characteristics (where they've come from, age, education level, etc.) change over time. A snapshot of today's migrants would look quite different from a similar picture taken ten or twenty years ago.

In recent years, the world has been awash in unprecedented numbers of migrants. Modern transportation, cheaper and more widely available than it has ever been, enables more people to migrate farther from their homelands. At the end of 1993, nearly 20 million refugees lived outside their native countries, most of them in developing nations. An additional 24 million were displaced from their homes inside the borders of their nations. The World Bank estimated in 1992 that, altogether, world migrants—refugees, migrant workers and their families, and others—totaled 100 million. Who are these migrants? Some are refugees from war or disaster. Some have migrated to find work. Some seek to settle permanently in a new country; others plan to return someday to their original homelands.

Increasingly, whole families migrate, not just individuals. In the 1960s and 1970s, male workers typically migrated alone, but by the 1980s many family members were following along. Today, worldwide, women and men migrate in nearly equal numbers, with most women in most regions migrating to find work—or to escape unbearable conditions at home—rather than simply to follow family.

Converging Reasons for Migration

POLICY makers in the United States and elsewhere try to draw sharp distinctions among those fleeing political oppression (entitled to asylum), refugees from natural disasters (deserving of humanitarian assistance), and migrating workers (liable to be shipped back whence they came). But developments around the world have blurred these distinctions and challenged us to come up with new ways to respond to migration.

Increasingly in many places, reasons for migration are converging and compelling great numbers of people to leave their homelands. Haiti—described here in the 1980s—is a vivid example of how complicated and urgent the reasons for mass migration can be:

Haiti, already the poorest country in the Western Hemisphere, also has the fastest-growing population. One third of the nation's land, exhausted by decades of deforestation and poor husbandry, is now virtually useless, and about 40 percent of the population is malnourished. More than half of the land is held by less than 4 percent of the planters. The average holding for a peasant farmer is less than an acre.

When food production per person began to decline in the fifties, farmers began adding to their incomes by selling charcoal. As trees vanished, so did the topsoil, further reducing food production and increasing reliance on charcoal for income. A combination of political repression, economic decline, and environmental devastation has pushed an estimated one million refugees—one sixth of Haiti's population—out of the country over the past decades.

Jodi L. Jacobson
Worldwatch Institute, 1988

Is the typical Haitian migrant fleeing pervasive political violence, a collapsed economy, or an overpopulated and bankrupt natural environment? Probably all three.

Economic Migration

WHEN an area's population grows faster than its economy, people will leave in search of work and a better life. This kind of migration is not new. Over the past century and a half, for example, so many people have left Ireland for the United States that there are far more people of Irish descent living in the United States than in Ireland.

An unprecedented number of people around the world are migrating today at least partly for economic reasons. Over the past half century, income per person in wealthier countries has tripled while it has remained flat in poorer countries. This has created a powerful incentive for many people to migrate. The world's two main magnets for economic migration in recent years have been western Europe (which attracts migrants from southern and eastern Europe as well as from northern Africa and the Middle East) and North America.

The United States attracts economic migrants from all over the world, but especially from Mexico. Not only does Mexico share a long border with the United States, but its economy offers workers compelling reasons to migrate: In the 1980s Mexican workers' productivity rose while wages *fell*; wages began to rise again in 1987, but by 1993 they still hadn't recovered even to 1980 levels.

Demographic Pressures

WORLD population is increasing fast: The number of people on this planet grows by about 90 million each year. During 1992 world population reached 5.5 billion, and it is expected to reach 10 billion before leveling off in the next century.

This staggering population growth is concentrated in the less-developed areas of the world: Africa, Asia, and Latin America. Infant mortality has dropped considerably in even the poorest countries in this century, but birthrates in most of the developing world have not dropped so much, so the populations of these countries are disproportionately young. Even if these countries' birthrates drop, their populations will continue to grow for two or three generations, while all those young people—and their children—raise families.

In Mexico, for example, the average number of children born to each woman throughout her life had—by 1993—been falling for nearly a generation. But because of the higher birthrates of earlier years, the work force continued to grow by a million people a year. (In contrast, by the 1990s only two million new workers were being added each year in the United States, which has a population almost three times the size of Mexico's and an economy nearly thirty times as large.) Rural and developing economies can't absorb all the young people entering the work force each year, so young people migrate in search of work—from rural areas to cities, and from less-developed regions to the developed economies of Europe and North America.

Rural-to-Urban Migration

RURAL areas throughout the world have been experiencing changes—not all of them economic—that push people off farms and into cities. These changes include: population growing beyond what local farms can support; investment in large-scale agriculture that reduces the need for farm labor; a decline in opportunities and services in rural areas compared to cities; livelihoods derived from traditional grazing, fishing, forest, and other common rights being lost to private property interests; pollution and erosion cutting agricultural productivity.

By the early 1990s, 20 million to 30 million of the world's poorest people were migrating from rural to urban areas each year, while the urban areas of the developing world couldn't provide enough services or economic opportunity to keep up with their growing populations. Millions of migrants leave these overflowing cities each year for countries that offer greater economic opportunities. Some have come to the United States; many more would like to.

Rural-to-urban migration is unevenly distributed around the world, and regional factors have a great impact on it. In Africa, for example, the widespread acquired immune deficiency syndrome (AIDS) epidemic tends to kill people in their most productive years. This has further weakened already fragile economies, families, and health and social security systems in the areas hit hardest and has spurred migration to cities.

In Latin America and Asia, rural-to-urban migration has slowed recently, and most urban growth now comes from children being born in the cities. Nonetheless, the migration that has already taken place has been so massive (Mexico City, for example, grew from 3.5 million in 1950 to 18 million in 1992) and the populations of the developing cities are so young that they will continue to grow rapidly for many years, even if rural migration slows to a trickle.

Environmental Pressures

OVERPOPULATION and careless development cause or worsen many kinds of environmental damage: deforestation, soil erosion, desertification, and especially water contamination and shortages. These problems are not new: As long ago as 2500 to 2000 B.C., in the Middle East, powerful Sumerian city-states collapsed because centuries of intensive, unsustainable irrigated farming had destroyed the land's ability to feed a growing population.

A stressed environment is more prone to catastrophe—and overpopulation pushes people into catastrophically risky situations. Draining wetlands and cutting forests make floods more extreme; more people living in a floodplain means more people left homeless when the floods come; houses built on deforested hillsides are vulnerable to disastrous mudslides.

Environmental degradation (damage that reduces an ecosystem's ability to support life) swells the number of migrants in many categories: victims of drought and other natural disasters made worse by previous human-caused damage, internal migrants who have exhausted the resources of one patch of land and must move to another, rural-to-urban migrants, refugees from civil conflicts aggravated by competition for ever-scarcer resources, and victims of technological disasters, such as the tens of thousands forced to leave their homes in the area around the failed Soviet nuclear power plant at Chernobyl. The number of such migrants that we see today may be much smaller than what we'll see in the future. Perhaps as many as 50 million refugees would be set adrift if global warming were to cause only a one-yard rise in the level of the world's oceans.

Political Pressures

POLITICAL crises, by themselves or in combination with population pressures, economic incentives, and environmental degradation, can also generate waves of migrants—or close off migration routes, leaving large numbers with no place to go. Wars in Africa, Southeast Asia, and Central America have all set waves of migrants adrift in recent years. The 1990–1991 Gulf War uprooted perhaps two million migrants from Asia and various Arab states who had been working in Iraq and other Persian Gulf states. And the collapse of the Soviet bloc and the disintegration of Yugoslavia have let loose a mass migration of millions toward western Europe.

The experiences of several refugees from the civil war in Somalia, who came to the United States in 1993, illustrate some of the difficulties experienced by even those war refugees lucky enough to find safe and stable new homes:

Transplanted from the bleak but familiar chaos of the refugee camps to an alien and often indecipherable city . . . they were greeted by strangers and left in a neighborhood [in Washington, D.C.] where they knew no one.

"That night I never forget," [Mohamad] Hussein said of his introduction to [his new home] in June, which marked the end of an odyssey that began 24 hours earlier in Kenya. "We don't know anything. I open the door. They say, 'This is your home.' . . . They give the key. They say, 'See you tomorrow.'

"How's up? How's down?" he said, trying to explain the disorientation he and his wife and nephew felt. . . .

"We were so afraid. It was a dark night. . . . All we are saying is Allah will save you. Maybe tomorrow." . . .

Like . . . most of the other Somali men, Hussein was accepted as a refugee because he had worked at the U.S. Embassy in Mogadishu. He spent seven months in a refugee camp in Kenya, waiting for a chance to emigrate and find what he vaguely hoped would be a better life. His apartment, like that of other refugees, is now furnished with castaway furniture. The bounty includes an old crushed-velvet sofa and chairs and the best curbside find yet, a 12-inch Goldstar television that he and another family share. *"Two nights here. Two nights upstairs,"* Hussein said.

The need for money and services is a constant preoccupation. . . . Refugees get a stipend of about $5 a day for the first three weeks, until emergency food stamps are available. By the beginning of the second month, they should receive a welfare check and regular food stamps. They are then expected to pay a share of the monthly rent. . . . After eight months, all federal aid ends, and they are on their own.

The Washington Post
November 28, 1993

Where Do They Come From, Where Are They Going?

MANY countries sheltering large numbers of refugees are among the world's poorest; the refugees are often from war-stricken neighboring countries. Thailand, for example, in 1991 hosted half a million refugees from Indochina and Myanmar (Burma); Pakistan and Iran took in six million Afghans in the 1980s; and in Africa, Malawi by the end of 1991 had accepted nearly a million refugees from neighboring Mozambique.

A few Asian countries—Japan, South Korea, Singapore, Malaysia—have attracted migrant workers from other Asian countries to work in their expanding economies. (Some of these migrants stay longer than they're welcome: 280,000 foreigners overstayed their legally permitted visits in Japan in 1992, up from just 20,500 in 1989.) Most Asian nations, though—especially the Philippines, countries in the Indian subcontinent, South Korea, and Vietnam—export large numbers of laborers to nations all over the world. The largest nation, China, restricts emigration but has the potential to unleash more migrants than any other nation:

The work force in China right now is about 580 million people, roughly 160 million of them in urban areas, and the rest in the countryside. But out of that 400-plus million in the countryside, less than 200 million are needed on the farm. And so they've got this surplus population in the countryside of 200 million, plus it is growing by 20 million per year. What do they do with these people? They've started rural industries that are doing very well but they absorb roughly a hundred million people. Okay. What do you do with the other 130, 140 million people? Well, what they've done is they have allowed them to drift towards the coast to the big cities looking for work.

James McGregor
The Wall Street Journal
November 9, 1993

Of course, there's not enough work for these people in the cities either, and many seek ways to emigrate illegally.

In Africa, especially western Africa, a great deal of migration has traditionally taken place within particular regions, and this flow continues. But civil wars and war-caused famines have forced millions of additional Africans to migrate in recent years. Most of these migrants have remained in Africa. In southern Africa, migration along the established path to work in South Africa has decreased. But from northern Africa, record numbers in recent years have migrated to western Europe.

About 15 million migrants entered western Europe between 1980 and 1992. Some were from Africa and Asia, and most recently huge numbers have migrated from the former Soviet Union and Warsaw Pact states and from the war-torn former Yugoslavia. Formerly Communist states in eastern and central Europe that have very little experience dealing with immigration are now receiving large numbers of migrants, from within their region as well as from developing nations.

Latin America sends many migrants abroad, and Mexico tops the list of the region's sending countries (Colombia is second). Virtually all of the migrants from Mexico go to the United States, legally or illegally.

The United States, of course, draws immigrants from all over the world. The mix and numbers of immigrants admitted to America have changed dramatically over the years—and so has the complex set of rules devised to regulate immigration.

Holding Onto My Cultural Identity

from Newcomers to America

Judith E. Greenberg

Many immigrants struggle to find a way of adapting to American culture without losing ties to their native lands. Here, young immigrants discuss the ways in which they balance their complex cultural identity.

Yetta

NOW I keep my culture alive by how I live. I visit my family. I have my grandchildren and my beautiful great-granddaughter who is gorgeous. If I don't see her for a few days, I miss her. When I was younger, I invited all the family to holidays at my house and we were all very close. We took care of each other and never forgot to help each other and remember hard times and good times together. I wish for my great-granddaughter to be a grown-up girl. I wish to see her start school. I wish it was twenty-five years back and I was a younger woman.

Miki

ESPECIALLY in the last few years, I have established contact with Czechoslovakia, and with the disappearance of the Iron Curtain, I have been able to go back and establish ties with my family there. Now I see that a person can be universal; I guess I think that way because I was born in one place and raised in several other places, and am now settled in the United States. I guess I probably do have some ties, nevertheless. I celebrate Thanksgiving and feel very American in the sense that I am in-volved in the politics and care about who is elected and why they are elected. On the other hand, well, I felt a great deal of happiness when the revolution took place in Czechoslovakia.

Maureen

THE Irish culture isn't super different from the American when it's all said and done. Of course, I have always loved Irish music and literature, and I have a tremendous number of books on Ireland. I like Irish music, but I love music so much in general that I listen to all types of music. But I don't like the way the Irish culture was portrayed and still is to some extent.

Now, I am not Catholic, but you know, in Ireland on holidays, no matter what religion you are, you have the day off from school and people were religious all their lives. It's like Easter or Passover, on our religious holidays schools were always closed, but they are not anymore. In my childhood, people didn't wear green clothes—that was considered clownish, like going around in a red-white- and blue-striped suit. So you just don't wear bright things. Now [in America] on St. Patrick's day, people wear green clothes and are absolutely horrified that I am not wearing anything green. I say "Why?" They say it's St. Patrick's day, and I try to explain that people don't do that and nobody believes me. And then this thing about people serving and drinking green beer—I am just appalled. My aunt and uncle just laughed at it, and said it is kind of a distorted view of a national holiday, that it was no big thing—but, it's weird. It's so different and it's mindboggling the way it is portrayed.

Chandler

WE have a lot of friends from our country, you know. We get together every weekend, somebody usually throws a party. We have a lot of friends and they always have birthday parties with the kids, but for any special occasion they have a big party gathering, too.

How did living in the United States change me? I have changed myself not much at all. I am still the same. I don't think I have changed, same easygoing person, the culture is much the same. I would say I have more opportunities here to go into business.

Ann

BECAUSE I work two jobs, I am so busy and by the time I get home, it is time for me to prepare to go to work again tomorrow. The only day I used to have off was Sunday. We all live together, eight of us together. Because my mother is busy with grandchildren, it is my father who does the cooking. And, he cooks mostly Chinese.

Now that we are a little more settled, we have all kinds of activities, for example, New Year's, Christmas, any kind of holiday in my country. We always have a good time. People are very warm over there, we have a good time. Here everybody does their own celebration, they only do family. In my country, friends and family relatives come together and have a good time all day long. Here they do their own way, quiet.

Enrique

I TRY to keep my culture alive because there is more of a need to practice it and to have people learn about us. Here you are competing with a lot of different races that are not necessarily your own, and there are a lot of people, many cultures all around. Yes, and cooking, traditional stuff and music, and language—you need all this.

Maybe I began feeling I was starting to fit into life here about five years ago. It took me ten years to adjust.

Carlos

FOOD, and music, and my friends and I go to museums a lot; these help me keep my culture alive. I do a lot of reading, anything that has to do with my country, I try to do this so that I do not lose my heritage.

When did I begin to feel that I was fitting into American life? I think in my twenties. I am twenty-four now. As I got older I was happy to be on my own, knowing I had to do whatever I must to survive. I think I felt pressured by my friends my age who were Americans, and who were doing what they were supposed to be doing—like getting a job and going to school. I wasn't.

I think living in the United States has changed me. I think I have become really caught up in trying to get an education, to try to grow intellectually. I mean I think this is really very good. Sometimes I think that a lot of the things that I used to value, such as family or sharing a meal, taking the time for eating together, I now resent because I feel I could be learning something, I feel that learning has become a priority above everything else.

Nilou

KEEPING a culture alive is hard. There aren't that many organizations in school for international groups, and I don't go to those. I really stay away from gatherings because I don't agree with a lot of their culture. I think I am partly Iranian, partly American—I don't know. We keep our culture alive by traditions and by the five holidays that we celebrate.

Yeah, I have changed definitely. In Iran, as a woman, I'd go to school, but universities are very hard to get into. In Iran I would have to get a job after high school and get married when I'm twenty or something. Most women don't work in very high positions, especially because the culture is very sexist. I'm happy to be here, the culture here is not sexist or is not sexist everywhere. Everybody is trying to be more politically correct here.

In schools there is a Spanish club, a Chinese club, but I don't know if there is an Iranian club. We are trying to make an Iranian club but I don't know if it will work, there are about eleven or twelve kids.

I think a club is a way of trying to keep the culture alive. In the Hispanic club, every Thursday, they get together and they dance, and on Tuesdays, they have meetings. I don't know what else they do, I know they dance Hispanic dances. We also have an international concert that we can go to and sing if you like, dance, bring food, you know, just whatever you want to do, whatever you want to present of your culture.

Some kids go to these clubs and dance and have fun, some kids think, well, why shouldn't we have a Caucasian club? The Irish, you know, they are getting out of it, saying, we should have our own club. Some kids get mad, but its pretty much okay.

About fitting into American life, when I came to public school I saw that America is really a melting pot, it is like borrowing things from other cultures—schools, building, furniture, everything from different cultures—and so, there is no American way. You can't look at people and say they look like Americans, because America is really borrowing from everything else and everybody is American and, that was when I realized I am American—because all Americans are different.

We should teach that people are people and everybody is the same, they just have different ways of handling their problems and different lifestyles, but we probably have the same goals.

I think that depending on what school you go to, it's getting more and more that way. We are studying African cultures and then Hispanic cultures. They teach us about other cultures more and more.

My friends are from all different parts of the world; my American friends are different, my Iranian friends are different, everybody is different, but the same too.

Gabi

NO I don't do anything special for my culture. My whole family is here, my parents. I guess we have picked up a lot of American culture, everything we do. Not that we think about it a lot, we just do it. Obviously, my mother makes Lithuanian breakfast at home and things like that.

I would have been totally different if I had not come here. It made me think about a lot of things. In my house I think I started looking at people differently because I have come into a totally different culture and I think I want to view people differently. I think I do view people differently. I still do a lot of things from my old culture, but as time goes by, I become more and more Americanized. I think I would have been a completely different person if I didn't come here. I am less sheltered and more worldly in my thinking.

Fassil

HERE, in the metropolitan area, there is a very large number of us. I would say approximately 30,000 to 40,000. And there are a lot of parties and things going on at different times, and also there are a lot of churches we can go to—I would say about fifteen or sixteen of them are around. So we are always in touch with the community. I have two children, a fifteen year old and a twelve year old. I am responsible to see they participate (in the community).

Living in the United States has changed me. You become exposed to a lot of things just by living here. You can learn a lot about life, a lot of things, but you pick up different customs and you are aware of other types of people.

Erika

I NEVER tried to forget where I came from or what I am, and at school it was very easy because I had many friends who would speak Spanish. All day I used to speak Spanish, the only time I would speak English was with the teachers when I had to work. That's why I speak very little English, because I don't practice. At school we used to have a Latino program. We used to dance for old people. We prepared a Spanish dance and went with a group to dance, it was easy to do that. But now that I am out of school, I don't have much time to go to church. We do celebrate our holidays but American holidays too.

Well, sometimes I think about going back home, but first I want to have a career. I don't want to go back there and just be nothing. And I study here and do something for myself. I plan to stay here and live my life here. I can have more opportunities here than in my country, in work, everything. More kinds of jobs, everything.

Anna

MY family and I still celebrate all my home holidays and all the American holidays too. We have family reunions and eat the basic cultural foods at home. This is very important. Because I was older when we left, I can always remember my country and the way of life. But my little sisters were not as old and it is necessary to make sure they learn and keep a part of their heritage, really as much as possible, alive. My aunt has an African-style clothing store and my uncle is back home in Liberia so we get magazines from Liberia to help us keep in touch with styles and trends there. That helps with the clothing store too. I like all kinds of music and I listen to the music of my country too. I also keep my culture alive by joining clubs.

I think I started to feel more like I was fitting into the American way of life when I started college and got a job. I have worked in retail and in marketing, and met many people who were clients. I relate well to people now and am not so frightened! I spend a lot of time with friends from college and do not feel so different because there are many people from outside the country here in school.

Alice

I DID not keep the culture alive at all when I was young. As a matter of fact, because I was taken away from it, I killed it. I didn't want to think about it once my mom said to me no, you're not going back. My grandmother was planning to move back to the Virgin Islands at that time, she was planning, so I told her I didn't mind going back with her because I just wanted to live in the Islands—it was closer to Nevis. My mother said no, you are not going. So we moved from New York to Connecticut and I was raised in New Haven. There are a lot of Caribbean people there but they are much older. They migrated years ago, went to school with the Americans. I had only American friends. I became fully Americanized. That's how my culture did not exist anymore. I lost it totally.

There were so many things I had never known, people would ask me where were you born? I knew nothing about the place I came from. I was a misfit and that was it. I would volunteer at cultural things because I wanted to find out more about them because I became very interested in connecting again. So now I'm involved totally. More Caribbean than American, I get into all the cultural activities and constantly promote my country, even linking up with the other Caribbean countries. I'm very

very much into it. I am the only family link to the Caribbean culture right now, the only link. The rest are not involved at all, they are not even interested. I am the only one who goes back home two and three times a year and goes to other places. I will always go back to the Caribbean; they won't and they are very much Americanized.

Soo

KEEPING my culture alive is easy. I work in a Korean church with a pastor and with many English-speaking Asians. It also includes Asian-Americans and people of other ethnic backgrounds. We are very exposed to Korean people at other churches, the largest church is about 3,000. We come into contact every week with other Asian people.

Even though we are English speakers, it's not strange for us to speak Korean. My wife and I speak Korean very well, we try to show the children Korean designs to help them to do alphabets and grammar. We will take them back to Korea if we can afford it, take the family for a vacation back to Korea.

I don't want my children to lose their Korean identity and their legal names. For instance, when they were born, I gave them English names, Nicholas and Nelson, but their middle names are the Korean name. I want to leave that in their minds and in their lives, even on their documents, that their identity is Korean—not to say that I don't want them to be fully American. They will be, but I know that when they grow up they will one day go to work and just like I was asked, they'll be asked what they are. It's Italian-American, British-American, Polish-American, and so on.

The Fields

W. S. Merwin

Saturday on Seventh Street
full-waisted gray-haired women in Sunday sweaters
moving through the tan shades of their booths
bend over cakes they baked at home
they gaze down onto the sleep of stuffed cabbages
they stir with huge spoons sauerkraut and potato
    dumplings
cooked as those dishes were cooked on deep
misty plains among the sounds of horses
beside fields of black earth on the other side of the globe
that only the oldest think they remember
looking down from their windows into the world
where everybody is now

none of the young has yet wept at the smell
of cabbages
those leaves all face
none of the young after long journeys
weeks in vessels
and staring at strange coasts through fog in first light
has been recognized by the steam of sauerkraut
that is older than anyone living
so on the street they play the music
of what they do not remember
they sing of places they have not known
they dance in new costumes under the windows
in the smell of cabbages from fields
nobody has seen

Reply to the Question: "How Can You Become a Poet?"

Eve Merriam

take the leaf of a tree
trace its exact shape
the outside edges
and inner lines

memorize the way it is fastened to the twig
(and how the twig arches from the branch)
how it springs forth in April
how it is panoplied in July

by late August
crumple it in your hand
so that you smell its end-of-summer sadness

chew its woody stem

listen to its autumn rattle

watch as it atomizes in the November air

then in winter
when there is no leaf left

        invent one

Acknowledgments *(continued from p. ii)*

Henry Holt and Company, Inc.

Letters From Rifka by Karen Hesse, © 1992 by Karen Hesse. Reprinted by permission of Henry Holt and Company, Inc.

Houghton Mifflin Company

"Would You Like a Star Too?" by Ida Vos from *Hide and Seek* by Ida Vos, translated from the Dutch by Terese Edelstein and Inez Smidt. © 1981 by Ida Vos. First American Edition 1991. All rights reserved. Reprinted by permission of Houghton Mifflin Company.

Millbrook Press

"Ukraine's Troubled History" from *The Handbook of the Former Soviet Union* by Michael G. Kort. Copyright © 1997 by Michael G. Kort. "World Migration in the 1990's" from *Immigration: Newcomers and Their Impact on the United States* by Tricia Andryszewski. Copyright © 1995 by Tricia Andryszewski.

William Morrow and Company, Inc.

From *Such a Life* by Edith LaZebnik. Copyright © 1978 by Edith LaZebnik. Reprinted by permission of William Morrow and Company, Inc.

Marian Reiner

"Reply to the Question: How Can You Become a Poet?" by Eve Merriam, from *Rainbow Writing* by Eve Merriam. Copyright © 1976 by Eve Merriam. Used by permission of Marian Reiner.

Note: Every effort has been made to locate the copyright owner of material reprinted in this book. Omissions brought to our attention will be corrected in subsequent editions.